The Properties Director's Handbook

The Properties Director's Handbook

Managing a Prop Shop for Theatre

Sandra J. Strawn

Focal Press
Taylor & Francis Group

NEW YORK AND LONDON

First published 2013
by Focal Press
70 Blanchard Rd Suite 402 Burlington, MA 01803

Simultaneously published in the UK
by Focal Press
2 Park Square, Milton Park, Abingdon, Oxon OX14 4RN

Focal Press is an imprint of the Taylor & Francis Group, an Informa business

Notices
Knowledge and best practice in this field are constantly changing. As new
research and experience broaden our understanding, changes in research
methods, professional practices, or medical treatment may become necessary.

Practitioners and researchers must always rely on their own experience and
knowledge in evaluating and using any information, methods, compounds, or
experiments described herein. In using such information or methods they should
be mindful of their own safety and the safety of others, including parties for
whom they have a professional responsibility.

Product or corporate names may be trademarks or registered trademarks, and are
used only for identification and explanation without intent to infringe.

Library of Congress Cataloging in Publication Data
Strawn, Sandra J.
  The properties director's handbook : managing a prop shop for theatre/Sandra
J. Strawn.
    p. cm.
  Includes bibliographical references and index.
  1. Stage props—Design and construction. 2. Theaters—Stage-setting and scenery.
I. Title.
  PN2091.S8S763 2012
  792.02'5—dc23

                              2012035625

ISBN: 978-0-415-66327-4 (pbk)
ISBN: 978-0-203-06638-6 (ebk)

Typeset in Berling
Project Managed and Typeset by: diacriTech

SUSTAINABLE
FORESTRY
INITIATIVE

Certified Sourcing
www.sfiprogram.org
SFI-00555
The SFI label applies to the text stock.

Printed and bound in the United States of America by
Walsworth Publishing Company, Marceline, MO.

Table of Contents

Introduction

Theatre has been an important part of my life for nearly three decades. Working in the prop shop, managing a show, creating a world onstage— this rewards the dedicated prop person in ways unimaginable. The collaboration with other artists and designers creates a community of creativity and possibility rarely experienced by other artistic practition- ers. In the theatre, we are bound by the script, defined by the design, and open to every possibility within our imagination. We collaborate to produce the elements of time, place, and character. In production, no part stands separate from the others, and in the coming together of cos- tumes, lights, sound, scenery, and props, we define the world on stage.

This book explores the process of being a properties director, manag- ing a prop shop, and leading the build on a show. Like all management, it's about the efficient use of resources—time, money, and people. In theatre, layered on top of being a manager of a shop and the people who work in it, the properties director fulfills the design team's chal- lenge through imagination, craft, and skill-based experience. Working in a nonprofit theatre, one's wealth is not measured by the amount of salary made but by the challenges overcome and the work created. The world can use more artists, more dreamers, and more folks who can think, "What if ...?" Come join us.

I teach properties design and production classes at the University of Wisconsin–Milwaukee (UWM). I was a professional properties director/ artisan (Actors Theatre of Louisville, Milwaukee Repertory Theatre,

Guthrie Theatre, and Utah Shakespearean Festival) when UWM recruited me to develop the props training track in the Professional Theatre Training Program. My theatre students arrive with an interest in technical theatre having hung lights, built scenery, or run a show in high school or community theatre, but few are familiar with props. Each class of students sifts out a gifted few who excel in the props area, and many of these folks go on to successful professional careers.

As my students learn the skills and techniques to work in a prop shop, they often wish for a textbook on how to be a prop master. Books are available for teaching many of the skills of a prop artisan—sewing, casting and molding, furniture construction, metalworking, plastic work, floral, and craft work. What my students want is a handbook to guide them through the entire process of managing a prop shop and a show build. Originally available as a webpage, prophandbook.com, this book explores those far more intangible skills of being a properties director for the student, prop professional, and prop enthusiast.

My continued deep appreciation for content assistance and general editing goes to my close friend, *Lisa Schlenker* (Properties Director, Skylight Opera Theatre) who was a strong advocate for my writing a webpage for properties directors and encouraged me in the writing of this book. *Mary Kay Stone* (Prop Master, formerly of Cincinnati Playhouse) offered helpful suggestions and encouragement in the writing of the webpage.

Numerous people have contributed in a variety of ways from offering suggestions about content, allowing photos to be taken in their shops, contributing forms and documents, and lending a supportive voice. My appreciation for cheerful willingness to be interviewed and provide information/assistance goes to:

Mark Walston (Properties Director, Actors Theatre of Louisville)
Doc Manning (Properties Master, Actors Theatre of Louisville)
Lisa Schlenker (Properties Director, Skylight Opera Theatre)
Jolene Obertin (Properties Director, Seattle Repertory Theatre)
Rick Gilles (Properties Director, Dallas Theatre Center)
Elizabeth (Freed) Friedrich (Properties Director, Intiman Theatre)
Marne Cohen-Vance (Properties Master, A Contemporary Theatre)
Edie Whitsett (Properties Director, Seattle Children's Theatre)

Jim Guy (Properties Director, Milwaukee Repertory Theatre)
Cindy Lee (Properties Director, American Repertory Theatre)
Members of Society of Properties Artisans/Managers (SPAM)

Deep appreciation goes to George Abraham for his enduring patience and goodwill as I have worked these many months on finalizing this project. Special thanks to my son, Jacob Garst, for letting me help on all his school projects and Halloween/Cosplay costumes over the years and who gave me computer lessons so I could create my webpage, eventually leading to writing this book. My webpage was made and this book was written on a Mac.

Chapter 1

What is a Prop?

Props live in the world of the visual design created by the scenic designer used to establish the stage setting for the play. They are the details fleshing out the architecture to define the characters in the play, set the time period, support the action needed within the structure of the play, and complete the "bridge" between the characters on stage and the reality of life objects.

A good analogy to define "What is a prop?" has been likened to the real-life situation of when a person moves from one home to another. A moving van pulls up and all the contents of the home are loaded in the van and it drives off to be unloaded into the new house. The house is the scenery. The scenery includes the actual walls, floors, ceilings, and doors—the architecture of the house. This does not move. It is stationary and permanent. The items boxed up, covered in pads, and carried out to the moving van when a person is changing residences would all be considered the props.

The props are all the nonpermanent items. Think of what would be put in that moving van—dishes, lamps, chairs, books, pictures, furniture, blankets, drapes, rugs, letters, office supplies, appliances, lawn tools—all the "stuff" people need in their everyday living and utilize to furnish their homes. It can be either personal (a book on Egypt) or nonspecific (a pillow), but every item says something about who owns that item. Even the nonspecific pillow tells us something. Is it

FIGURE 1 Hand props used to support the action of the scene, *Arms and the Man*, University of Wisconsin–Milwaukee.

a bed or sofa pillow? Feather or foam? In a pillowcase or ticking cover? Clean or stained? Each item is a small clue to who the owner is, giving insight into the character of the owner. Making the choices about what it all looks like and finding or building those items is the prop person's job.

Props can be broken down into several easy categories, and most prop shops work with three categories: set props, hand props, and stage dressing.

A *hand prop* is anything carried or handled by an actor within the action of a scene. It often helps define an actor's specific character such as a cane, cigar, liquor flask, lipstick, feather duster, floral bouquet, or sword. A hand prop might also help fulfill the action described in the play such as a gun used to threaten another character, a fountain pen for signing a contract, a letter opened and read, or a piece of fruit eaten and enjoyed.

Making a hand prop list can be done specific to character or listed just as they appear within the play. The script might mention numerous props on first read through but hand props are the one area that seems to change the most depending on the rehearsal process.

The "adds" of hand props arrive as the play is being blocked and worked through in the initial staging process. Actors will often make specific requests for a hand prop they need to help them in "fleshing out" their character. This is also the area getting the most "cuts" in the final weeks of rehearsal and "tech" as the action of the scenes becomes more comfortable and the actors sure of their characters.

Making an initial listing of the props and being able to analyze a script to find the props start the prop build process. Read the script for both items and action.

In the example below from *Seven Guitars* by August Wilson, Act I, Scene 4, some of the hand props are called out in the character dialogue, whereas other props are simply implied.

LOUISE: *Ohh. Just the man I want to see. Give me one of them Old Golds. Hedley give me one of these old Chesterfields. Here I'll trade you the pack.*
RED CARTER: *Naw. I ain't gonna do that. I don't want no Chesterfield! I don't see how people smoke them things.*

From these two lines, the hand props would include a pack of Old Gold cigarettes, a pack of Chesterfield cigarettes, and possibly matches or a lighter to light the cigarettes (making them a consumable) and maybe requiring an ashtray.

When making the listing, it is handy to group items together going to support a single action or character even if it may not be called out in that particular scene or mentioned in the script. For example, if you have a character who asks for a cup of tea, the props required to support this single request might be as simple as a mug of tea. On the other hand, it might be a full tea service on a tea cart complete with silver trays, serving teapot, cups, saucers, sugar bowl with silver tongs and cubed sugar, a small cream pitcher, tea spoons, waste bowl, and tea caddy. Although the character only mentions a cup of tea, it may be appropriate to support the request in a more complete and visual way. In addition, it is helpful to ask other questions: What fits the action? What fits the length of dialogue? Do they have time to make the tea? Should the tea already be made in the teapot? Is it appropriate for the characters to own and use a tea service? Or, is this just a request for a mug of tea? The director or designer will need to answer these questions, so have a list with appropriate questions for the initial design conference. Some questions may need to be taken to stage management and solved as the play is rehearsed.

FIGURE 2   Furniture pieces used to set the scene for Act II, *Ring Round the Moon*.

The *set props* are the large movable items that are not built into the set and are used to help establish place. Generally, this is the furniture or "sittables" and would include things like chairs, tables, rugs, appliances, barrels, trunks, or large rocks. But it can also include larger items like tents, a canoe, a car, or even a wrestling ring. Research photos showing style or finish and/or drawings for pieces to be built are communicated to the prop shop directly from the scenic designer. Their size and location is notated on the floor plan showing the relationship within the stage setting and used by stage management to set up for rehearsal purposes. The initial description of the setting is often communicated from the playwright at the top of the scene.

It may be a sentence as simple as this one from *Proof* by David Auburn:

SETTING

A back porch of a house in Chicago

This description gives little information about the props needed or the time period. The details are placed throughout the script itself in the action of the characters needing places to sit or picking up objects and relating to items on the stage. To prepare for the first meeting with the designer, the properties director would need to read carefully to get an understanding of what set props might be required.

On the other hand, some playwrights give quite complete visual descriptions with specific prop information such as in *Seven Guitars* by August Wilson.

SETTING

The action of the play takes place in the backyard of a house in Pittsburgh in 1948. It is a brick house with a single window fronting the yard. Access to the room is gained by stairs leading to a small porch on the side of the house. This is VERA'S apartment. LOUISE and HEDLEY live on the second floor in separate quarters, which are accessed by steps leading to a landing and a flight of stairs alongside the building. The stairs are wooden and are in need of repair. The yard is closely flanked on both sides by the neighboring buildings. A ten-foot high fence stage right blocks our view into the yard a stage right and a four-foot high fence is at stage left. The yard is a dirt yard with a small garden area marked off by bricks in the downstage right corner where VERA has made a garden of vegetables and flowers. A cellar door leads into the basement where HEDLEY stores his gear. Off to the side and in the back of the yard is a contraption made of bricks, wood, and corrugated sheet metal which is where Hedley kills chickens. It couples as a grill for cooking and when it is not being used, it breaks down with a minimum of parts left standing. During several of his scenes HEDLEY builds or dismantles his contraption and stores its pieces in the cellar. There is an entrance to the yard through a latched gate to the left of the building. There is occasionally a card table set up in the yard with an eclectic mix of chairs. Several light bulbs, rigged by way of extension cords, run from VERA's apartment to light the table so they can sit and play cards on the hot summer nights of 1948.

The prop list can be started from this description. Set props would include the card table, chairs (various), and the chicken killing contraption/grill.

Both of these script examples are for plays set in the back of a house in the city, but the level of information provided on props varies considerably. The scene designer may use this description as the basis for the design or may choose to completely ignore it, but at least it's a place to start understanding what may be required to set the scene. Once the design has been finalized, this information is often communicated to the prop shop directly from the scenic designer, and size and location is notated on the floor plan showing the relationship within the stage setting.

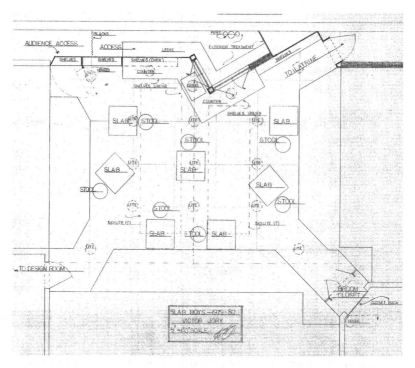

FIGURE 3   *Slab Boys* floor plan with prop notation for set props and dressing. Courtesy of Paul Owen, Scenic designer, Actors Theatre of Louisville.

Set props tend to be fairly well defined early on because that information is needed before rehearsal begins. They may also take up the bulk of the budget and the energy of the build in many shows, so it's helpful to know this information as soon as possible from the designer allowing preliminary budgeting for the build to happen. Furniture pieces set time period and character quickly, and hence, the prop shop must find the specific items requested by the designer for a particular look. The challenge lies in also finding the piece with the right look that will also function well for the action as defined in rehearsal by the director. In addition, the pieces often have to be shifted and moved to show a passage of time or to allow for a scene change between places. Prop furniture takes a high level of abuse, and often the actions blocked on the furniture puts more stress on a piece than it would normally receive in a lifetime or normal use in a home environment. Appropriate reinforcement and finishes must be considered as items are selected or built.

Working from what is available in stock, designers may choose to have items built or altered specifically to fit the show. Utilizing photos or sketches, the designer communicates the "look" desired to the prop shop, and the prop build begins.

FIGURE 4 Pillows, magazines, a cigarette box and lighter on a tray, a lavish floral arrangement, and bar glasses and bottles dress the set for *Hayfever*, University of Wisconsin–Milwaukee.

Stage dressing encompasses all the decorative items used to enhance the visual setting. These items are rarely moved or even touched by the actors and are mostly used to help the designer establish place or time period as well as character detail. Examples would include curtains on the window, books in a bookcase, hanging chandeliers, a moose head hanging on the wall, magazines and floral arrangements spread on a coffee table, or pictures arranged on a wall. Although dressing may be mentioned in the script, it is rarely complete and usually ignored as the designer determines the details to fit with the particular design being created for the specific production.

Stage dressing information usually comes from the designer and may be communicated to the prop shop in various ways. Often the designer communicates the look desired by simply describing what is needed and relying on the prop shop to fulfill expectations from that verbal description. This works best in relationships where the prop shop and designer have worked together enough to have a strong understanding of what the designer means and usually envisions. Understanding and getting "into the head" of the designer to *see* what the designer is seeing as the vision for the play makes the verbal design process easier. It is sometimes easiest to talk about set dressing by utilizing the scaled model of the stage setting or from the front elevations. Some designers include highly detailed stage dressing in their models. Others

FIGURE 5   Set model for *The Gin Game*, designed by Paul Owen, Actors Theatre of Louisville, showing furniture style and placement, suggestion of set decoration and foliage requirements as well as color and texture choices.

take front elevations and overlay prop detail onto the drawing showing size or placement of pictures, sketching in draperies, or showing other dressing detail. Working with the elevations or the model even while talking with the designer assists in clarifying what the designer is imagining.

The smaller, detailed stage dressing is often just a conversation between the designer and the properties director talking about what might be placed around the stage. For example, if the play takes place in a modern apartment with a bookcase, coffee table, credenza, TV and stereo cabinet, sofa, and other decor, the designer may call out for several specific items of decoration, but will assume that the prop shop would fill the bookcase with appropriate books and collectable items, dress the coffee table with magazines fitting the characters and season of the play, cover the credenza with a small decorative runner topped by a vase of flowers or piece of sculpture, file CD's and record covers in the stereo cabinet beside a remote control for the TV, pull throw pillows and a soft blanket for the back of the sofa, and otherwise make the setting appear like someone actually lives in the space. The selection and set dressing of those props is left up to the discretion of the props department although most designers will "tweak" the final dressing to suit their personal vision.

For decor such as curtains or furniture pieces, designers often utilize photos or drawings to show fullness, drape, trim elements, pattern, color, etc. From this collage of images, the prop shop works in collaboration with the designer for the purchasing of specific fabric, trim, or items to re-create the look.

Stage dressing can also include large items such as trees, grass, bushes, or other landscape items falling almost over into set props. These items might be considered scenery in some theatres. As in all things, negotiation and collaboration are essential in determining who is responsible for building the various parts of the production depending on budget, talent, and time.

Properties production, of all the areas in the production side of doing theatre, is probably the most collaborative with the designers and director. Although some information is available from the drawings that designers produce and from rehearsal, the prop shop often researches and creates much of what is placed on stage directed by their sense of the overall design sensibility and an understanding of

FIGURE 6 *Hayfever* stage setting before set dressing. Note scenery delayed-missing molding and final floor painting. Kurt Sharp, Scenic Designer, University of Wisconsin–Milwaukee.

FIGURE 7 Preview set shot with furniture in place, hand props preset, and completed stage dressing on walls and furniture pieces. Note dressing in backing areas of garden, front door, and upstairs hall. Kurt Sharp, Scenic Designer, University of Wisconsin–Milwaukee.

time period, and place and an interpretation of character from the rehearsal process.

Adding the furniture props and stage dressing is what brings the space to life. Props bridge the space between the actor and the setting, making it human and bringing it alive, giving it dimension, color, character and offering clues to the world of the play.

Chapter 2

Who Does What

The prop shop lives in the hierarchy of the theatre organization. It is only one of the legs in the multiappendage creature called "production" needed to mount a show successfully.

The evolution of the properties position is murky, and it is only in the last few decades the status of having someone directly responsible for the props has been codified. In the past, too often all the props were left to whoever could scrounge together the list of items needed, and anything needing to be built was requested from the scene shop or costume shop who did it around their other priorities. Sometimes stage managers were required to find props as part of their job of supporting the rehearsal and performance process. Today all that is changed. The prop shop is a separate entity working in a close collaboration with its cohorts in costumes, scenery, electrics, and sound.

The person who manages the prop shop goes by various titles depending on the theatre organization itself. Many regional theatre properties shop are managed by the *properties director* and accountable for the on-time, on-budget, as-designed production of the stage properties to the satisfaction of the scene designer.

The use of the "Master" name as in properties master and master electrician was commonly used when the technical director was the overall head of the technical production process. The movement to the properties director title is an evolution most dominant in the last decade, as the technical director became the person who managed the scene shop and

FIGURE 1   Prop Director Jim Guy talks with Props Artisan Sarah Heck, Milwaukee Repertory Theatre.

the larger managerial position overseeing the entire production budget, personnel, and calendar was titled production manager. The title of properties director was utilized to acknowledge the separate and equal nature of the work between the prop shop and scene shop and the equal footing of the job with the technical director.

Some smaller companies have a different line of accountability with a technical director coordinating all the production areas, and in those cases, the person who manages the prop shop is often called the *properties master* or *properties manager*. The title of properties master is a "traditional" title and is used by some as a nod to historical convention even when the job duties and accountability structure are identical to a properties director. In theatres with an International Association of Theatrical Stage Employees (IATSE) contract for the running of the shows, the Union prop person might also be called the properties master, but would not be responsible for managing the prop shop or working on the actual build. It just depends on the particular person and theatre organization.

In recent years, the title of *properties designer* has evolved in acknowledgement of the higher level of collaboration that the prop shop has with the scenic designer in creating the complete stage setting. Some designers utilize the properties designer to complete the majority of prop decisions and design the details fulfilling the overall intention of the design just as, in the past, an assistant designer might have fulfilled those requirements. However, the properties designer has the management and process skills needed to move those design choices directly into the shop, whereas the assistant designer position often just created another level of communication to manage in the build between the prop shop and the designer.

The properties designer works in collaboration with the scenic designer to design the properties as a part of the design team. The properties designer must then make the design decisions evolving during the rehearsal process meeting the needs of the particular scene/actor/script problem. The properties designer addresses those concerns and allows the changes to be considered into the overall design of the show as set by the scenic design. Having the properties designer in-house as the head of the props area facilitates a quick response. This is especially true when a theatre company utilizes freelance scenic designers who may be juggling a number of shows and are unavailable to make daily input into the design/prop build process.

Even when no properties designer is designated, it seems many scenic designers are relying more and more heavily on the properties director/prop shop manager to make design decisions based on an understanding of the overall look of the scenic design and in collaboration with the director. It is common in many companies to give equal billing in the program to the properties director along with the other designers in acknowledgment of this creative activity and collaboration.

SKILLS

The *properties director* must have a strong background in management of a shop and staff, budgeting, period research, be able to read, interpret, and draft the scenic designer's prop sketches into working drawings utilizing appropriate construction techniques/materials to satisfy the production's particular needs, be skilled in all phases of property construction, and be a collaborative and effective communicator with stage managers, directors, actors, and other area heads. The properties director is responsible for maintaining the prop shop tools and equipment and keeping a wide variety of supplies in stock from lumber, steel, plastics, and paint to sewing and craft materials.

The properties director establishes and maintains the high standard of safety for work done in the shops and on stage. Although each person in the prop shop, and indeed in the theatre, is ultimately responsible for insuring their own safety and making personal decisions about work processes and products used in the production of theatre props, the properties director should make safety a top priority. Beyond just the obvious desire to work in a healthy and safe environment, it's the law. The general duty clause of The Occupational Safety and Health Act states, in part, that the employer shall furnish "employment and a place of employment which are free from recognized hazards." The properties director has an obligation to maintain health and safety standards for the protection of all who work in the shop and to promote necessary tool/supply upgrades and shop maintenance needed to comply with safe working practices to both the management and the prop staff.

Most importantly, the properties director manages the build as it moves through the shop, adjusting crew assignments and determining priorities in response to rehearsal requests, availability of materials, changes in the prop list, difficulties in building a prop, and all of the juggling of whether some particular prop is built, bought, pulled, or borrowed from another company. Attendance at production and design meetings allows for efficient communication with all departments including those overlapping into props such as costumes, scenery, or electrics. Acting as the point person in the prop shop, they direct necessary information to the properties crew about changes in specific props or projects, to stage management about status of projects and specific handling or use of props, and to the designer about requested changes or rehearsal adds. They also work with the production manager to balance the budget needs for the show and the personnel hires.

In addition to running the prop shop, the properties director is often responsible for the maintenance of the properties stock and managing prop rentals to community organizations and other theatres. The Marketing and Development office often requests assistance from the prop shop for backstage tours, educational events, fund raising galas decoration, photo shoots, and other community and fund raising events.

In small theatres and especially at the university and community theatre level, the properties director is often a one-person shop. Obviously, the level of production must also be smaller given the limited number of hours in the day and the ability of one person to do the work accomplished by a full staff in other organizations. The one-person properties shop usually relies on strong local contacts for borrowing items and a realistic understanding of the limitations necessitated by budget, time, and availability of volunteers or other production personnel who may be able to help out if they have time available in their own production work. However, the passion and commitment demonstrated by these small shops remain the same for the dedicated properties director striving to put on stage the best product to support the play.

THE PROP STAFF

Most regional theatres and larger producing organizations have a staff to support the prop build. Assisting the properties director is a crew of *properties artisans*. They are responsible for the construction, acquisition, and innovative creation of all props used in a production. Small shops have artisans utilizing a large variety of skills with the expectation that each person has the skills to move the prop from beginning to end through the shop. Larger shops tend to have specialist artisans who work exclusively in their area of expertise such as soft goods artisan, carpenter, crafts artisan, shopper/buyer, or assistant prop master/prop shop manager.

Properties artisans work under the supervision of the properties director but are expected to be creative, innovative, collaborative artists honoring the design intent while making the props stage worthy and safe. The properties director may also delegate some responsibilities to the artisans such as the maintenance of tools, purchasing of supplies, management of stock, etc.

A *soft good artisan* completes the patterning, draping, tailoring, and sewing of fabric-based projects. An understanding of fabric and sewing techniques is a necessity. Upholstery projects

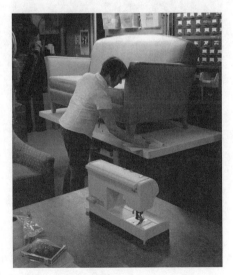

FIGURE 2 Soft Goods Artisan Margaret Hasek-Guy at Milwaukee Repertory Theatre.

utilize theatrical techniques duplicating traditional looks, but often utilizing many of "costuming" tricks for fabric use. Sewing skills are required to build the pillows, curtains, bed coverings, drapes, and all the various "soft" props needed. An understanding of fabric dyeing and distressing is important. On shop-built items, the soft goods artisan works in the design and construction part of the project to prepare the frame for the soft goods work.

A *properties carpenter* works to construct, restore, conserve, or alter furniture and other items from wood, plastic, or metal for the stage. Using construction techniques similar to theatrical scenic construction as well as traditional woodworking processes, prop carpentry skills must allow for the repair of damaged or fragile original pieces to a stageworthy status, reinforce stock pieces appropriately to protect them for specific stage action, and modify existing pieces to create a designed or specific period silhouette and structure. Increasingly, properties carpenters also fabricate furniture from scratch to meet specific design requirements as an alternative to purchasing an expensive antique and attempting to strengthen the old piece for stage use. An understanding of finishing techniques and detailing is important as well as skills in metal work and welding to construct reinforcing armatures or ornamental pieces.

FIGURE 3 Props Artisan/Carpenter Jen Lyons builds a roulette table for the Skylight Opera Production, *La Traviata*.

The *crafts artisan* is truly a jack of all trades and should possess a wide variety of skills including casting and molding, graphics layout and manipulation, faux painting, floral arrangement, leather working, jewelry making, special effects, carving, and sculpture work. Larger theatres may have a person hired to specifically fill the crafts position to supplement the specialty artisans who often have crafts skills complimenting their area of specialty. This position may also be shared with another area such as costumes or the paint shop depending on the skills of the person.

The *shopper/buyer* finds and procures the products, raw materials, requested items, or specific props needed for the build of the show. Good visualization skills and an understanding of process are especially important as this artisan must coordinate the acquisition of what needs to be purchased with the other arti-

FIGURE 4 Crafts Artisan Anna Warren models clay to build a statue resembling the actors face portraying a historical figure on Milwaukee Repertory Theatre's stage.

sans who are using those items to build the props. Strong interpersonal skills help in negotiating purchases and setting up delivery of goods as well as just in the location and purchasing of items. An understanding of budget management and accounting is important in coordination with the properties director who is managing the overall budgetary decisions. Strong computer skills for research and acquisition are especially valuable in this position as the ability to find specific items or order materials has become more accessible via the web and eBay purchasing, making the entire world a prop market place.

The position of *assistant prop master* or *prop shop manager* is found in larger theatres where multiple shows may be in the prop shop requiring a mid-level shop manager to solve day-to-day shop priorities, while the properties director juggles the overall management of all the shows. The assistant might also be assigned to the management of a single show within the build of multiple shows in a shop.

Hand Props Skills

Calligraphy
Model making
Graphics layout
Molding/casting
Jewelry making
Quilting/embroidery/knitting
Papier-mâché
Leatherwork
Musical instrumentation
Painting—spray paint techniques, acrylics, watercolors, colored pen and pencil
Culinary/food preparation
Weaponry/pyrotechniques

Set Props Skills

Sewing
Welding/metal working
Furniture construction/restoration
Woodworking
Plastics construction
Upholstery
Draping/fabric layout/pattern making
Fabric dyeing/distressing
Faux painting—wood grain, marble, stone, aging
Radio control/pneumatics/small specialty electronics
Special effects
Plumbing

Dressing Skills

Painting—acrylics/watercolors/portraiture
Floral arrangement
Sculpture/3D carving/foam carving
Electrical construction/wiring
Picture matting and framing
Photography
Shopping
Pulling from stock to fit the show

A good prop person is truly a "Jack (or Jill) of All Trades." Every hobby, interest, or experience adds to the body of knowledge informing the skill set of a props artisan. Just think of all the situations represented on stage and the various characters portrayed needing to have props to help them fulfill the action of their character or to define something about their person. Every day events coupled with an observant and curious mind can form a body of knowledge needed to replicate similar events on stage. The key is to assemble a staff having an eclectic, varied, and balanced group of skills, interests, and strengths, so no matter what is thrown at the prop shop to solve, one of the groups can step up and say, "Oh … I know how to do that …."

Beyond the hands-on skills, a good prop person must be flexible in their work process as priorities change and props get added or cut. They must be creative and able to see how to adapt and modify items to

Sensibilities of a Prop Person

Organization
Time management
Flexibility in the work process
Diplomacy
Collaboration
Creativity
Eye for detail
Flair for design
Color coordination
Textural sympathy
Creative adaptability—seeing "What if …"
Drafting/sketching/graphic communication
High production standards
Self-motivation
Innovative thinking
Research inquisitiveness
Computer expertise—word/spreadsheet/drafting/graphics
Memory for details/sizes/history/visuals
Safety awareness and compliance

create something new or different. Prop people must have an eye for detail and flair for design utilizing color coordination and textural sympathy in interpreting the designer's ideas. High production standards supported by an understanding of how things work on stage demand innovation and a passion for doing this very specialized work to create props meeting the design parameters, produced in a timely manner, and working within the budget restrictions.

CONTRACTS AND SALARIES

Contract length and salaries of prop staff have evolved along with the definition of job titles. Salary is determined by many factors including size of the organization, length and complexity of the season, historical precedent, geographical location, and health of the organization. If the theatre has a contract with IATSE (International Alliance of Theatrical Stage Employees), those union salaries are determined by negotiation, and nonunion employees not covered in those negotiations will probably be impacted by those pay scales. Contract length is determined with many of the same factors in mind as well as reflecting specific show builds when more or less staff is required. Mid-season "furloughs," when the season is lighter and less staff is required to produce or run the shows, are a common tool, which drastically impacts the yearly salary for employees.

Depending on the internal accountability structure, many properties directors are making a comparable wage with the technical director and other departmental heads. The properties director is an "administrative" or "artistic" position and is not usually a part of an IATSE contract. Due to it's salaried nature, overtime is not usually granted, so during tech and load-in weeks, although the hours spent at the theatre may double, the salary remains the same. Those shops with IATSE contracts who have staff earning overtime soon see the staff earning more than the properties director during "crunch" times when the hours in the shop increase. In the 2012 survey of prop shops across the United States by *Society of Properties Artisans/Managers* (SPAM), the national organization for prop directors in the United States, the *average* weekly salary for a properties director averaged around $750 weekly making just over $40,000 a year. Top tier theatres with full-year contracts pay over $55,000 a year and provide full benefit packages including retirement, vacation days, and health care coverage. Smaller theatres or companies in smaller markets pay far less and employ the properties staff for less than full-year contracts. Yearly incomes for prop directors at those organizations range as low as $18,800 a year.

Properties artisans are in the same range for salaries and contract lengths as a scenic carpenter or costume artisan. Staff hours during nontech weeks are commonly 40 hours a week with an additional 10–30 hours during load-in and tech week. Although many properties directors are now full-time staff with yearly contracts, most prop artisans are hired on contracts ranging between 28 and 42 weeks with an equally wide range of salaries. The *average* salary is $608 weekly for a props artisan. Beginning level artisan salaries start around $475 a week (2012 survey—SPAM). Many artisans employed at top tier theatres in major urban centers make over $45,000 a year and receive full benefit packages.

The hourly rate for nonsalary staff had quite a wide range from $11.00 an hour to $24.80 with the *average* being just over $18.00 an hour (2012 survey—SPAM).

Most theatres offer some form of overtime pay or compensated time off for hours worked beyond the 40-hour week. The trick is finding time off within the contracted season to make up those "comp" hours without impacting the next show build. All too often overtime hours worked are never compensated equally to the time earned.

Those shops operating under an IATSE contract negotiate the pay with the local representatives, and the rate varies from theatre to theatre, but generally is within a close range in a city. Union rates vary widely depending on the city and availability of work. Union workers are paid an hourly wage and are paid overtime for work over the standard 40 workweek. Some contracts may set the workweek differently. Most Union contracts pay at the top end of the hourly range for nonsalary staff.

Larger LORT (League of Resident Theatres) companies obviously pay better in acknowledgement of the additional administrative responsibilities and the size of the season. Smaller theatres with shorter seasons and many summer theatres pay far less than the average, making it a challenge to survive financially without doing side work for other theatres; having a second job outside of theatre in retail or other better paying occupation or finding ways to supplement income as an independent artist, designer, or craftsperson using the same theatre skills in a different way.

Benefits are available to many full-time and contracted season staff including health and dental coverage, disability insurance, some form of a retirement plan or investment savings plan such as a 401K, and vacation/sick days. Some companies provide other benefits such as a free parking space, use of the shop for personal project work, complimentary tickets to productions, and reimbursement for personal use of your car.

FINDING WORK

Finding a properties position is commonly done by word of mouth with people seeking out others they know and advertising openings through e-mail distributions and web sites. Most large organizations also utilize publications such as *Artsearch* or online job listing services like Backstagejobs.com. Theatres also advertise openings on their own webpages under a Staff or Employment Opportunities header. Networking to find out potential openings or to discover any upcoming staff expansions is always helpful. It's also a good way to find out relevant information about job descriptions, salaries, benefits, organizational structure, and culture. The world of props is small, and the players are known to each other by professional connections as well as being active in national theatre organizations such as USITT (United States Institute for Theatre Technology) or SPAM (Society of Properties Artisans/Managers). Word of mouth and a recommendation by a credible theatre maker opens many doors and, given the turnover in staff at many regional theatres, beginning level jobs open up with some regularity as people advance in their careers. Having the right set of skills and a passion for the craft of properties production is the first step to finding and growing a career in props.

Many prop masters working at the leading regional theatres came to the position by working up from assistant positions. Some started as interns and slowly moved up the chain of responsibility; others as actors or designers, but found their passion in the prop world. Every experience makes a better prop person.

BEGINNING A PROP CAREER

A beginning level position found in many organizations is the *properties intern*. An internship in the prop shop of a regional theatre is one of the best ways to make the move from theatre training at a university to the professional theatre world. Many educational institutions offer classes for credit in the final year of the training curriculum supporting an internship for either a full or partial semester. Professional theatre companies offer internships knowing they are preparing the next level of craftsperson to be hired into the profession. An internship exposes the student to professional work processes and products building on whatever level of training was offered in the university. By engaging with craftspeople, designers, and directors in the professional environment, the student learns professional work standards and develops the professional contacts necessary for a successful career within the theatre industry.

In a recent SPAM survey of both regional and summer theatres, 38 regional theatres offered some form of an internship with many offering a small stipend or other financial support. Of the 23 *summer* theatres responding to the survey, most offered a stipend as well as housing.

Most interns are expected to work the same hours as paid staff and may be assigned as an assistant to a full-time staff member or even given individual projects to complete depending on the skills of the individual. Some theatres offer a hands-on training component in addition to just working in the shop. As the intern demonstrates ability and learns the way of working in a particular organization, opportunities to work on larger projects usually are given. Beyond learning professional technical skills, the intern is also exposed to the communication, organization, and leadership qualities needed to be successful.

To find an internship, search the web sites of the regional or summer theatres. Many have links available describing the opportunities for employment. On the theatre webpage, look for a link under a header such as Opportunities, Employment, Jobs, Education, Training, or Internship. Contacting the theatre in person or by phone is also a good way to discover what internship possibilities are available or who the contact person is for setting up an internship. If a particular theatre does not have an internship program in place, it is always possible to talk directly with the properties director about setting one up. Few theatres will turn away free labor, especially someone with an interest in the technical field who has some level of training and a passion for the work. Theatres with Union contracts may be limited in offering contracts due to their particular agreement with the local stagehands contract.

Accepting an internship carries with it the same responsibility of accepting a fully paid position. The staff of the prop shop will expect the intern to be engaged, collaborative, and hard working. In exchange, they offer the start of a successful career. An internship should not be viewed as a way to just see what goes on behind the scenes of a professional theatre, but must be approached as an entry-level job with the same consequences of success dependent on assessment and review by supervising personnel.

EDUCATION AND TRAINING

Learning how to be a prop person can be as varied as the prop process itself. Many of the people working in prop shops across the United States were trained with a general theatre background and developed their prop skills on the job. Others came to the prop shop from fine arts, woodworking, architecture, or other related "craft" training track. Some may only have a passion for theatre and a knack for the crafts work done in the prop shop.

Given its developmental track as an outgrowth of the scenery or costume shop, only a few universities offer props as a specific *undergraduate* training curriculum. They offer classes in properties production as well as specialty classes in soft goods/upholstery, casting/molding, woodworking/furniture restoration, or properties crafts. Several of the better known are University of Wisconsin–Milwaukee, North Carolina School of the Arts, Webster University, Syracuse University, and Ohio University.

In a recent survey of over 116 US universities and colleges, almost half offered at least *one* undergraduate class in stage properties. When considering a university curriculum, it is important to review past class catalogs (often available online) to see how often props classes have been taught and who taught the class. Most universities have classes in stagecraft or costume crafts teaching some prop skills, and certainly most of what is taught in a costume curriculum or a scenery construction

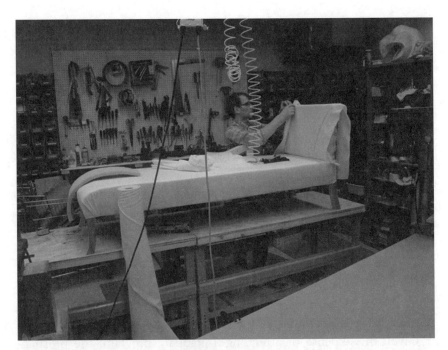

FIGURE 5 Props Carpenter Jay Tollefsen works on a chaise for *Hayfever*, University of Wisconsin–Milwaukee prop shop.

curriculum is adaptable to work in a prop shop. By examining the listing of classes, it should be possible to develop a well-rounded props curriculum from courses teaching dyeing and painting, millinery, sewing skills, carpentry skills, welding and metalworking, drafting, rendering techniques, design and decor, costume crafts, etc.

A prop student may also find classes offered in other departments around campus teaching skills and processes directly applicable to props and be able to build a curriculum supplementing theatre offerings. Classes available in art departments might include sculpture, drawing, painting, jewelry, textiles, and computer graphics. Architecture departments offer classes in interior design and drafting, as well as furniture design. Some colleges have industrial design classes teaching wood, plastic, and metal production classes, with "hands-on" shops for project work. Exploring the class catalog can open up a wide array of opportunities to build a custom prop training curriculum.

Graduate degrees are offered in professional theatre training programs in Production Technology or Technical Direction. They offer properties classes as part of the general training curriculum. The programs at North Carolina School of the Arts and the University of Delaware offer at least two classes in properties production skills. California Institute of the Arts lists a Properties Design, Management, and Construction track in their MFA (Masters of Fine Arts) curriculum with a wider variety of props classes from Prop and Puppetry techniques to Advanced Prop Design and Set Decoration.

Graduate prop programs are available at University of Illinois (Urbana–Champagne) and Louisiana State University that also offer assistantships and scholarships. As in all things, it is wise to review the curriculums and class offerings to see how often classes are taught and the credentials of the person teaching the class. A graduate level degree is not required for a properties job in regional theatre, although many of the advanced degree programs not only teach some of the hands-on skills classes, but also focus the training on developing the administrative and leadership abilities of the graduate student.

Given the expense of attending a graduate program, the prospective student should consider what would be the best investment of time and money. Having a scholarship or assistantship to pay tuition and other expenses becomes almost mandatory unless adequate self-funding is possible. Graduating with a heavy debt load from graduate school training is an enormous burden considering the salaries of most theatre professionals. Many prop people interviewed believe the hands-on training found in the profession to be of equal value as a graduate training program, and gave them the on-the-job access to promotions needed to have a successful career.

Although not all organizations have a separate designated prop shop, a staff of prop artisans, and dedicated budgets for props, the process of properties production remains the same. No two prop shops are run the same way or have the same balance of skill in the personnel. Every build is different given the variables of when it falls in the season, who is designing, who is directing, what is available in storage, who is available to work in the shop, what is the budget, etc. However, understanding the *process* and *procedures* for properties production discussed in these following chapters should help any organization to have an effective and collaborative properties production experience.

Chapter 3

Preproduction and Planning

It all begins with the *script*. For props, the script defines the world of the play establishing the setting, the characters, and the action. Reading the script or analyzing the score, in the case of a musical or opera, is the first entry into what the props will be for the production.

The first read of the script should be for basic understandings of the story, i.e., who are the characters and what is happening in the play. This read is critical to having a framework of understanding for the flow of action in the script and a summary of the plot and characters.

On the second and third read through, finding the details becomes more important. Where is the play set? (city, building, specific room, country). When is the play set? (season, period, time of day, holiday time). Who are these characters? (jobs, economic status, social status, relationships, passions, fears, religion, family group). What happens in the play? (actionable event, supporting events).

For example, in *A Different Moon*, written by Ara Watson, in Act II, the following scene occurs:

SARAH: *(Entering) I think maybe I better sit down in here for …*
RUTH: *Let me.*
SARAH: *I'm fine. I'm only …*
RUTH: *(Leading her to sofa) Well, of course you're fine. Now, you sit down right … (seats her) … there. Would you like a cold washrag?*
SARAH: *No … I'm really … It was just all the smells … made me …*

RUTH: *And I've had that stove on and it's hot in there ... Would you like to lie down? I'll get you a pillow if*
SARAH: *No. Thank you.*

(Ruth makes a quick exit into the kitchen and reenters immediately with a plate on which are two pieces of toast)

RUTH: *Here you go. You nibble on this and you'll feel a lot better. (Puts the plate down next to her) I know what I'm talking about. (Sarah takes a piece of toast and takes a small bite.) You just sit right there and eat your toast.*

and later in the same scene

SARAH: *I like your house. You've got real nice furniture.*
RUTH: *Thank you. Mostly odds and ends. This table, though ... I'm fond of this table. This one. It belonged to my mother. All hand carved by her brother. (She touches it lovingly.) And these two chairs are from her dining room. There were eight of them and we—my two brothers and my sister, myself—each took two. I got the two with the side arms.*
SARAH: *They're real nice.*
RUTH: *(Moving to a picture) This is my family.*
SARAH: *I saw that picture.*
RUTH: *(Picks up the picture and moves to Sarah) It was taken not long before my mother died. She was a really beautiful woman all her life, but ... cancer. (Looks at the picture and shakes her head, then more brightly.) This is my sister Leah—she lives in California— and this is my brother Wendall—he lives here in Masefield, runs the post office—and this is Justin, my brother, he lives two houses down. I think Tyler looks just like him—same chin.*
SARAH: *Is that you in the back?*
RUTH: *(Laughs) Yes. I had everyone standing in front of me because I was eight months—It was right before Tyler was born. (Putting the picture back in its place.) I must get a new frame for this.*

These few lines pulled from the script give valuable hints into many things impacting on the design and eventually, the prop choices. The kitchen is immediately adjacent to the living room because the toast can be so quickly fetched and so the house is small. This size perception is supported by the comment about the heat from the stove. This will probably affect the scale of furniture and even require some "kitchen" dressing support seen through a doorway. The toast must be brought in on a plate (hand prop). The toast is eaten, making it a consumable. We know some of the furniture now; the lines ask if she wants to lie down so whatever she sits on must be capable of also supporting someone reclining (a sofa), and the toast is set on an adjacent table easy for her to reach, so probably a side table or coffee table of some kind. From the next conversation, we get the sense that the furniture is hand-me-down but nice. It should not match. One table is quite specific in description requiring hand carving. Two of the chairs must be dining room chairs with arms.

The photograph (hand prop) in the scene is also quite specific. It is a framed family photograph with at least five people in the picture. Two of the people are men, three are women—one elderly and one pregnant. The final line suggests the frame may be "dated," but it could also simply be a way of changing the conversation and nothing is really wrong with it. Script analysis is not always a literal description. From these 16 lines, we begin to see the characters and understand what their world might look like.

As the script is read, underlining or highlighting the props, making notations in the border, or writing questions about something occurring in the action having an impact on the props is the start of organizing a way of thinking about the show and preparing to talk with the designers.

Understanding the script before the first production/design meeting is critical to participating as a collaborative and supportive partner in the design process. Although the director and/or designer may choose to move the time period or alter the convention of presentation in other ways, knowing the initial script establishes the foundation for moving into a different interpretation.

Finding and reading the same translation or revision being produced allows effective preparation and will certainly change the prop list preparation, so it is always wise to ask for the specific script information especially in the case of older shows where the play might have several translations or a revised version. Know which specific script is going to be used and work from that.

After reading the script, the next step is to create a *preliminary prop list* compiling the prop information to use in the production and design meetings. The following would be helpful information to include in a preliminary list:

■   Act, scene, and/or page number in script where prop is mentioned
■   Prop item
■   Description as mentioned in script
■   Character who uses the prop
■   Questions for designer/director

The preliminary prop list should include adequate information to assist in discussions with the director and scenic designer about how the prop will be used, what it looks like (size, shape, color, etc.), or to prompt inquiry into what may be a crossover prop with another production area (i.e., Does the floor lamp have work as a practical? Do they turn on the radio making it light up on the dial and music heard from the speaker? Do they eat the food mentioned? Does the gun come from a pocket or a holster? Are we using blood, if so, how much, how delivered, and how to clean it up?).

The furniture/set props may be described in the playwright's scene notes or may have to come from an analysis of what the characters are doing and how they relate to the space and each other. If four characters are playing cards, it can be assumed four chairs and a table of some kind are required as well as various hand props like a deck of cards and possibly gambling chips, beverage glasses, an ash tray, cigarettes, matches, score pad, or pencil.

Hand props are defined specific to character and may be noted as part of the character description or can be found related to the action within the scene such as the card playing scene mentioned above. Those hand props not directly embedded in the script should be noted, but often are the first ones to cut because they were specific to the production "recorded" when the script was published and may not be necessary in the present production.

Stage dressing will come directly from the specific design, so unless something is noted particular to the action (e.g., a painting of a character

SKYLIGHT OPERA THEATRE PROPERTIES DEPARTMENT
2008-2009 Season
The Producers: Preliminary prop list with questions

Act/Sc /pg	PROP	WHO	NOTES
	Act One Scene One: Schubert Alley		
1.1.1	NT Times Crate with papers	dressing	several other empty crates
	Schubert alley dressing:		built in to the set/portable/sittable standable?
1.1.1	Usherette props:	chcro	flash light? Pile of programs? Anything else?
1.1.1	Programs, playbills	chcro	Number? Style?
1.1.2	Opening/Closing Night sign	technician	hand held
1.1.2	Ladder	technician	to flip opening night sign over to reveal closing night
1.1.2	Newspaper	Max	script specific text P.3. Perishable.
1.1.3	Violin	blind violinist	Practical???
1.1.3	cop props:		Gun? Billy Club? Other?
1.1.3	newspaper vendor props:		Satchel? Cart?
1.1.3	grocery cart	bag lady	
1.1.3	booze bottle in paper bag	bum	
1.1.3	playbills	nuns	sound of music
1.1.3	broom & trash can on wheels	street sweeper	trash can on a separate hand truck, or just a wheeled version of a trash can??
1.1.3	Sandwich Board with sow advertisement		wom? If so, by whom?, or just sitting on the side walk?
	Act One Scene Two: Max Bialystock's office		
1.2.6	office desk		style? Size? Color?
1.2.6	desk dressing		how much? How organized? What sort of look?
1.2.6	desk chair		on wheels??
1.2.6	small safe		on wheels? Size, color, type of door? Empty in 1.8
1.2.6	refrigerator		does it open? Practical inside light? Size?
1.2.6	old upright piano		Practical? Internal Wireless amp and speakers for sound designer control?
	any drapes on the windows or French doors?		
1.2.6	2 framed show posters		When Cousins Marry: the Breaking wind, etc.
1.2.6	Underwear on clothes line		attachment points? Number of pieces?
1.2.6	hot plate		
1.2.6	telephone		on desk?
1.2.6	old leather sofa		size? Style? Color?
1.2.6	cheap leatheretle briefcase	Leo	how full?
1.2.6	blanket of newspaper sections	Max	
1.2.8	cabinet with little old lady photos	Max office	some removable, including 5×7 hold me touch me photo
1.2.8	Umbrella	little old lady	
1.2.8	check	hold me touch me	made out to cash. Probably perishable

FIGURE 1 Preliminary prop list for *The Producers*, Skylight Opera Theatre. Courtesy of Lisa Schlenker, Properties Director.

in the play referred to within the dialogue of the play), adding stage dressing to the prop list at this early point in the process is unnecessary. It can be handy for prompting discussion with the director and designer, but usually these items are not retained consistently from production to production.

In any given show, one area that can become a sinkhole of expense is the *consumable* budget. A consumable is any prop requiring multiples to be made/purchased, because in the action of the play, the prop is used in such a way that it cannot be reused. It might be eaten, torn, broken, gotten wet, set on fire, etc. It can be as simple as an envelope torn open each night or as involved as the clock thrown on the floor and smashed in Chekhov's *Three Sisters* requiring the casting of enough clocks for the technical rehearsal and run the show. It could also be the entire kitchen full of set dressing as in *True West* by Sam Shepard where the play culminates in a typewriter being beaten to pieces with a golf club each night along with a large number of toasters. Beyond exploring the problematic safety issue for the actors and audience as bits and pieces of appliances go flinging off, the production and design team need to address the expense of finding enough toasters, typewriters, and golf clubs for the run and potentially re-dressing the set each performance due to breakage or damage.

Food is a consumable requiring appropriate and safe handling beyond just the expense of buying the food items itself. The odd piece of fruit or piece of bread can be easily solved, but some plays require food to be cooked onstage or meals eaten by the actors as part of the staging of the scene. Planning for this level of consumable must be accounted for at the preliminary stage in both budget and use, including preshow preparation and postshow clean up expenses. Those items anticipated to be "consumable" should be notated in the preliminary prop list for discussion by all involved.

RESEARCH

At the start of every build, just as reading the script and making a preliminary prop list informs the world of the show, doing *research* into what that world may look like is a helpful exercise. The pleasure of working in theatre, and especially in the specialty of props, is our world changes with every production. For those few weeks of the build, the prop shop "lives" in the time period, location, social rank, and economic status of the play. We need to know who these people are and where they live. The decisions made about what the props look like and the choices made to represent the furniture, stage dressings, and personal items of the characters onstage must reflect the scripts parameters as well as the sensibilities of the artistic team. In a theatre season, one show can be an Irish political drama set in the 1700s and the next a modern New York comedy of manners set in a upscale apartment. Having a basis of visual representation to those specific places and times is a good foundation for design collaboration and decisions.

With the production team together at the design meetings to talk through the show, the designer may present images or sketches reflecting some of the conceptual research done in creating the overall "look" of the play. The designer may move time period or place, or take the play into a specific viewpoint or style, informing the decisions made about what the props look like. Some designs are modeled after specific art movements or even specific artist styles. Some designs are more skeletal and others almost photorealistic in the duplication of place and time period. Some designers may choose to send research images of furniture or props to show a range of choices fitting into the play motif with little regard to time period but more concerned with color or shape. All these conceptual approaches challenge the properties director in solving the build process. Being prepared and knowledgeable about the look of a period and an understanding of the shape, line, fabrics, materials, furniture, significant events, etc. appropriate to the play is essential. Research develops knowledge of the options and assists the properties director on offering solutions. Ultimately, research simply presents the "actual," allowing the artistic process to move to the "desired"; once we know what it looks like, we can design what it needs to be.

For example, the play might be set in 1920 Germany and the character is leaving home. How big is a suitcase in 1920 Germany? What kind of handles did they have? Did it have straps to hold it closed or just snap locks? What is the suitcase constructed from—cardboard, soft-sided fabric, metal? How were they covered—leather, cloth, edge bindings? Did they have rounded edges or square corners? What were common sizes? Getting answers helps define the "What does it look like?" question. Having an image as that starting point jumpstarts the evolution from what is "known" into the world of the designer's imagination. The prop shop does not try to reproduce a literal 1920 German suitcase. It builds a suitcase that when placed on stage and carried by an actor playing a man in Germany in 1920, "fits" into and does not detract from the scene. The viewer accepts it as a suitcase in Germany in 1920.

Many creative folk work best as visual responders. A verbal description cannot show as quickly what a few pictures can illustrate. Pulling together an assemblage of images allows for easy discussions with the designer. It informs the selection of stock items needing to be pulled and altered. It defines the selection of fabrics and color of finish on painted or upholstered items. It demonstrates the availability of items able to be purchased or borrowed. All these images create the foundation for the choices made to build the show.

DOING INTERNET RESEARCH

Doing research into a specific period is as easy as a click of the keyboard into the Internet. Vast quantities of images are available through image search engines or on web sites. Today's image libraries with clear pictures and multiple views provide an easy and simple way of finding a plethora of sources for design and building decisions.

Most search engines like Google allow the user to specify between *Web* and *Images* on the top bar near the search window. If images are all that is needed, click on *Images* and only pictures of what is requested will be found. If webpages of vendors who might sell items of interest are required, click on *Web* and the search will locate web sites. These web sites may contain pictures or drawings equally as helpful as the *Images*. Utilize both ways of searching if one doesn't seem to be giving good results.

For example, if the show being built requires a counter of extravagant desserts set in a French café, most designers will simply request a display of French pastries to dress out the countertop and not draw out specific desserts to be built by the prop shop. By typing "French Desserts" into the *Images* search window, thousands of pictures of various pastries, pies, cakes, donuts, and other yummy goodies are available for the use by the props craftsperson to create prop desserts.

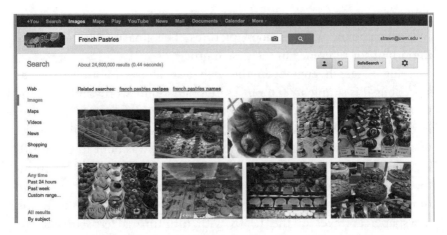

FIGURE 2   Images link on Google Search for French pastries.

A couple of more clicks through the *Images* pages and a quick scan down each page shows numerous photos of French pastry shops with extravagant displays of pastries showing how the display might be assembled, the style of the dressing, the various heights of the confectionary dishes, the dish styles, etc. Printing off these pictures and creating an assemblage of options allows the designer to select specific desserts or to define shapes, color, and textures working with the overall design. This information is shared with the prop shop staff and becomes the inspiration for the craftsperson to work in building the pastry display.

FIGURE 3   Web link on Google Search for French pastries.

If you were to type the same words into the *Web* search window, the listing becomes a long catalog of French cookbooks and recipes on online food sites as well as photos.

It is easy to peruse these for ingredients informing what the dessert might look like, and it is often helpful to have these directions almost as a method of construction or in the case of consumable props, to be able to cook the requested dessert. But if only fake desserts are needed, many web site cookbooks lack good pictures. The image is usually more important for reference in the design process.

Using a search engine on the web also allows for quite specific searching. It is simple to enter in a series of defining words and focus the search to match exactly with your research needs. If you were to enter in only "1950s, furniture," you would be shown furniture all over the world from the 1950s as well as furniture that was built in the 1950s for sale on eBay, modern furniture reflecting the look of 1950s furniture available at local discount stores or national chain stores, furniture timelines including the 1950s, historical information about the 1950s, newspaper archives of the 1950s with furniture advertisements, etc. Although fascinating, flipping through this can consume valuable research hours and fail to provide what you are ultimately trying to find, especially if you are looking for something specific.

However, typing in "1950s, metal swivel stools, American, drug store" delivers images for that specific stool type including examples of American drug store interiors, reproduction stools from vintage stores, and photos of people sitting on stools, catalog pictures of contemporary stools, etc. By flipping from *Images* over to *Web* and keeping the same search window terms, it's easy to locate furniture vendors who sell reproduction 1950s stools, collectible shops selling drug store paraphernalia, or an offering on eBay for a set of stools being sold from an old store. From there, it is a simple step to printing off the information or images and chatting with the designer about the choices available.

On many builds, it is a combination of uses of the web to find images and locate materials. For example, in *Seven Guitars* by August Wilson, a rooster is brought on stage and beheaded in each show. It must have the appearance of being quite alive for the gruesome act to have full impact and the actor uses the decapitated rooster's blood to mark a circle on the ground. To build this rooster (because an actual rooster being killed nightly on stage would have been highly impractical as well as overly bloody and enraging to the American Society for the Prevention of Cruelty to Animals), the prop shop needs information on the construction of a fake rooster.

Going online and downloading various images of "roosters" is easy. Click on *Images*, type in "rooster," and hundreds of pictures pop up giving close-up head shots, feet pictures, side views, chickens in a yard, roosters on a fence, state fair champion roosters, etc. The prop craftsperson knows what a rooster shape, size, wing to leg proportion, coloring, etc. all look like allowing the construction process to begin.

Next comes how to solve the "action" of the rooster, which needs to flop about, and what is more important, bleed on cue. Consider searching for "butchering chickens." YouTube offers a variety of short video clips showing people butchering chickens allowing the craftsperson to understand what action will need to be replicated. Maybe it can be done as a hand-controlled wing flap. So, type in "puppet controls" or "ventriloquist controls" to start the search for various methods of rigging the wings to flap. Type in "Special effects, blood" to be taken to sites showing ways to rig a fake blood delivery system.

Meanwhile, the prop shopper is searching online "taxidermy, chickens" for feathers, fake feet, or feather pelts for purchase. All this is available online. Today, research is only a click away showing what the chicken looks like as well as finding a taxidermist living in Idaho with cured full-size rooster pelts and additional pads of tail and breast feathers for sale, available to be delivered by FedEx for the craftsperson to begin building the fake rooster. This technology is revolutionizing the props process, and the world is shrinking as the commercial listings open up to anyone with computer access.

Walking in with a solution to the "rooster" problem (and there is something like this in almost every script!) with a ready solution or options for the designer and director to consider in those initial prop design meetings makes everyone's job easier and helps build a collaborative creative team.

PROP LIBRARY

Although researching on the web is easy and fast, most prop shops continue to maintain an extensive library of books from general history of furniture and style books to collectable books on specific items such as perfume bottles or fruit crate art. These in-shop libraries provide an invaluable hands-on trove of images and information. Having and knowing what is in the books make them a readily accessible source.

Having a huge wall of books, unorganized, and unread is a waste of space. Like all resources, for the library to be useable, it must be maintained and the users have to know the contents.

One of the best resources is an old catalog such as those printed by Sears Roebuck, JC Penney's, and other retailers. Mailed out since the turn of the century, each season new catalogs arrived all over America illustrating the entire range of products available for purchase. These old catalogs are still found in junk stores or second-hand bookstores and many prop shops have an extensive collection. Some reproduction catalogs are also available and original catalogs come up for sale on eBay with some regularity (search under: Vintage catalog). These catalogs offer a window into the everyday American world of clothing, household goods, farm implements, toys, travel, décor, and lifestyle. Detail in cost, availability, style, color, shape, trim, etc. is readily available through these books and the images contained within.

Other books of value focus on a specific time or items such as Victorian English interiors or American Federalist furniture. These books often help in giving a sense of style and décor as well as offering images showing the variety of what is appropriate to that time for the props.

Modern books on interior design that replicate a time period are also helpful as they tend to use many of the same theatrical shortcuts to interpret time or place that designers use. Lush photographs are often used to convey a certain look and can be a valuable resource in communicating an idea about fullness of drape, saturation of color choice, density of décor dressing, etc.

Photography books contain iconic images documenting time periods, events, people, places, and important historical events. Collections of photographs are published covering specific decades or about a specific topic such as the American Depression. Time/Life Books offers a plethora of books filled with images devoted to covering a variety of topics.

Art books provide imagery for the time period before photography was common. By studying paintings, the clues into how people lived are often revealed in the furniture, décor, clothing, and other items included in the artwork. Some designers choose to deliberately fashion a design in the style of a specific painter often from the time period the play was written. Having a book with the paintings of that particular artist makes many of the prop choices obvious.

Books written for collectors also show many pictures and have specific detailed information about country of origin, size, manufacture, ornamentation, etc. that helps in defining a specific prop. These are available in the most specific topics such as dollhouses, Belleek porcelain, comic books, toy soldiers, Native American art, jukeboxes, etc. Used bookstores or junk shops are a great place to find these books inexpensively and having them in the prop shop library is a quick way to access images on a specific topic quickly.

Public and school libraries, of course, offer an enormous resource of books available for checking out. Looking by subject matter such as "perfume bottles" may find a book on antique perfume bottles. If not, move beyond the obvious and look for books on collecting bottles, Czechoslovakian crystal, Tiffany, etc. It will take time and is usually no longer the first choice as a research method given the time constraints of theatre.

Depending on where you live, a local museum might also be a resource for research work. Most regional theatres operate in or near a major metropolitan city with fine art, natural history, decorative arts, and architectural museums available. Furniture, glassware, textiles, weaponry, and artwork are displayed for study and consideration. Take a step back in time in the permanent exhibits or explore a special collection relevant to the play. Most museums have an "education" department willing to allow special access, arrange for an opportunity to examine an object in closer detail or take a photograph for research simply by asking and obtaining permission. Having an actual object to take measurements from, to see the detail of joinery or finish, and to understand the fragility or weight of the item makes a trip to the museum worthwhile. Again, knowing the resource and having a contact to facilitate its use makes it valuable. Wandering around a museum hoping to find something you are searching for takes away valuable research time.

Research allows the prop staff to enter into the build process better informed about the time, the "look" of objects, possible pricing on available items, etc. Having done research before meeting with the designer and director allows an informed build process to be jump started and the prop shop to be working on completing the props with handy visual references or period information.

DESIGN MEETING

Once the preliminary prop list and research preparation is complete, a meeting with the designer and director is necessary to talk through the options of the props listed. When this happens will depend on the availability of the people involved. The sooner the better in most cases but at the very least this initial meeting should be scheduled several weeks before the start of the build. Some shops have the luxury of having these meetings months in advance allowing for a well-planned prop build, whereas other theatres may not have the information available until the start of the rehearsal period. Stage management usually attends the meeting to understand what considerations are discussed and to work out what needs to be facilitated in rehearsal.

Discussions revolve around all the details needed for the prop shop to begin the build. This is where initial decisions happen. For example, what do things look like, How are they anticipated to be used? What will need additional reinforcement? Where does it come from (out of a pocket, from offstage, flown in, out of a trap in the floor, from behind the proscenium, etc.)? How is it shifted (by stage crew, by actors, on wheels, on a rolling platform as part of the scenery shift, etc.)? What color is it? This information informs many of the additional decisions that will be made in the following weeks of the build.

It is important to note this is just the starting point and everyone involved acknowledges the prop list and design choices will evolve as things need to get added, cut, or changed based on the rehearsal process. It is also at this point where the overlap between departments often occurs depending on the priorities of budget, personnel, and talent. For example, what might have started out as a costume piece might slide over into props or vise versa depending on who has the time, money, or skill to complete the items.

Preparing for the design meetings may have various levels of effort. Once you get to know a specific designer and how they work, it's easy to match the preparation to the need. Some designers will come prepared with detailed photos and scaled drawings of the props; others will have nothing but a general scenic plan and little idea of what is necessary for the props. Regardless, it helps to have done the basic research into the more important items and to have a grasp of the time period of the play. The research information and images provide a visual communication tool utilized with the designer to select what the prop might look like. Often designers will pick and chose pieces of images to create a specific "new" image. The designer may communicate this information through a specific prop drawing, a collage style representation, or simply through verbal description based on a review of the available research, leaving the actual documentation process to the properties director.

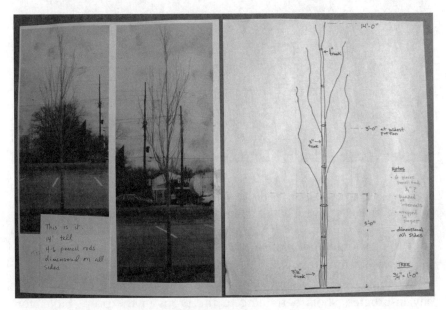

FIGURE 4 Research photos and designer sketch for tree.
Courtesy of Mark Walston, Properties Director, Actors Theatre of Louisville.

Compiling those images into a collage connected to a specific prop on the prop list gives the prop shop a way to direct the build on each item. It assists the budgeting process and defines the shopping priority for props needing to be bought or for defining the look of the fabric, trim, hardware, or raw materials necessary for an item to be constructed.

All research images/collages are assembled and stored in the *show "bible"* for access by the prop shop staff as necessary during the build. During the process of the build, when a question arises about how

FIGURE 5 Prop "bible" with design choices based on stock items, catalog choices, items for sale locally, and things available at other local theatres to borrow. Courtesy of Mark Walston, Properties Director, Actors Theatre of Louisville.

something should "look," the best answer is usually available by reviewing the research materials and designer notes.

Retaining show research along with the designer's notation and any in-progress shots pertaining to the props in the prop "bible" for documentation of the build is helpful for those shows that may be re-mounted at another theatre, sent out on tour, or are seasonal shows for annual remount such as *A Christmas Carol*. Having the source material makes additions to the show or replications in case of breakage or need for duplicates easier. It also allows the evolution of a prop to be tracked over several seasons when a different director uses the same scenic design for a seasonal show, but needs to alter the props to fit the newer version.

Preproduction script analysis and doing research give a foundation for the discussions and considerations during the entire build. As the properties director becomes engaged with the show and understands the particular interpretation and design statement determined for this production, all the information coalesces. This knowledge gives the properties director an armada of information on which to offer better choices and make appropriate decisions. As the prop shop begins the show build, knowing the script and understanding the historical and stylistic foundation, every choice becomes easier, and the prop shop can make the decisions to best support the designer's vision.

Following the design meetings with an understanding of what is needed from the designer and the director, a *prop list* is created combining the preliminary prop list and the information garnered from the production and design meetings. This list will form the basis of the build allowing the initial choice of what might be pulled, bought, built, rented, or borrowed to be determined by the properties director. From the prop list, the properties director is able to make a preliminary budget and anticipate any specific production challenges. And so, the build begins.

Chapter 4

Getting Organized

Keeping track of all the props requested by both the designer for the visual appearance and the director for the action of the play is the responsibility of the properties director. This is managed through the use of a *prop list*. The prop list should have every prop listed and a detailed notation of any details the properties director requires to track the prop or information about its use or look. Using a simple form to enter this information allows the management of "adds" and "cuts" and is a quickly accessed organizational tool. Most prop lists use column headers similar to this:

PAGE   TRACK #   ITEM/PROP   CHARACTER/FUNCTION
DESCRIPTION   ASSIGNMENT   ACQUIRE   STATUS

The *page number*, just as in the preliminary prop list, connects the prop being worked on to the specific page number in the script allowing the artisan to quickly find specific information. This is especially important when working on paper props where dialogue may be read from a letter or document. Copying exactly what is written in the script keeps the actor focused on the scene and prevents distraction. The page number reference is also a shortcut to finding how a prop is used when talking with a designer or in production meetings.

The *tracking number* is a simple tool for organizing the prop list. Many regional theatres use a numbering system, assigning each prop its own number allowing for effective tracking of the prop on all subsequent communications from rehearsal reports to build notes, load-in sheets, run sheets, etc. As props are added, each is assigned a number. Deleted props retain their number because all too often they return later in the process and can be easily added back.

Nonduplication or reassignment of a number also prevents confusion especially when prop lists are updated between the departments. Using a tracking numbering system is covered later in this chapter.

The *item/prop* column is a simple listing of each individual prop such as broom, chair, knife, or digital phone. The prop name should be kept the same in all areas of communication. Sometimes when similar items are used, a more descriptive name is given to a common item such as "wide handle basket" to differentiate that particular basket more easily from the other baskets being used. That name tracks through both the prop list and the stage management lists.

Connecting a prop to a specific *character/actor* or a particular "function" or "action" also helps clarify which prop the list is detailing. Entering the character name for a hand prop is helpful if the need to sort out hand props by individual occurs. For example, to find all the hand props for the character "Cyrano," the prop list can be quickly scanned for every entry in the column with that character name. Then a list can be made of all the props used by "Cyrano," allowing easy organization for rehearsal use or prop check-in by character.

The classification of "function" includes information on how the prop might be used, if it's a consumable prop, as well as notes communicating any idiosyncrasies of a particular item, for example, "fragile" or "lid pops off when dropped" or "not structural for standing on." It is also a handy place to note when a particular actor known for his physical use of props will be handling the prop so that special care can be identified.

A full *description* based on the information from the prop meeting with the director and designer (quantity, how it is used, color, size, detailing, etc.) and information on any research included in the "bible" should be notated in this column. Not all information needs to be included, but the listing should make the connection to whatever drawings, photos, research, or other finalized information is available. It is especially helpful to include sizing information as a quick reference guide instead of having to sort through the research pages for specifics when out shopping or in a meeting with stage management or others and a question comes up about a particular piece. Initially, this area might note any questions for the director or designer about the prop.

The prop list description also shows where overlap and collaboration with other departments occurs. For example, a chandelier requires the lighting department to run an electric cord for the needed power and the scenic department to rig a hanging line to suspend the fixture. The coordination of the project should be noted on the prop list to allow for adequate consultation between all areas. The prop list description area might have deadline dates noted for when it must be built for sending out to a specialty shop or when the piece needs to be in rehearsal.

As a management tool, the prop list also may have *assignments* for completion and a preliminary guesstimate of how the prop will be *acquired* (build, buy, borrow, and pull). Putting artisan names to particular props allows the properties director to balance the load across the shop, see where collaboration is needed, or determine whether a specialist/over hire situation is needed. Listing how the prop will be completed also shows where the shopper and the artisan must coordinate activity, the priority for pulling or finding props, and the obvious purchases the budget must allow. These definitions may change, but it gives a start to organizing the entire build. It is also easy to pull out each artisan's work list once names have been assigned or to create a *buy* list for the shopper, a *pull* list for the artisan going to prop storage, and a *borrow* list of the things needing to be found in the community at other theatres or organizations.

Finally, it's helpful to have a *status* column notating when a prop has been sent for use in rehearsal or what stage of completion it may have reached. A quick scan of the prop list allows the properties director to know when the prop has been used in rehearsal resolving many of the difficulties arising from first time prop use before even arriving onstage. Similarly, a notation of "waiting on fabric" or "paint" tells where the particular prop is in the process of the build and gives the properties

	A	B	C	E	F	G	H	I	J
1		**THREE SISTERS - Prop List**			Start of Rehearsal 2/19/12				
2		PROP MASTER: <u>MEREDITH ROAT</u>			DESIGNER: <u>SANDRA STRAWN</u>		DIRECTOR: <u>REBECCA HOLDERNESS</u>		
3									
5-6	Script Page	TRACKING #	PROP	CHARACTER	DESCRIPTION	AQUIRE B/B/B/P	ASSIGN	STATUS	x
7					**FURNITURE ACT I**				
8	3	F01	Desk	Olga	Borrowed from MKE Rep	Borrow	Ann	Paint	
9	3	F02	Desk Chair	Olga	to go with Desk F01	Pull	Ann	Upholstery	
10	3	F05	Bench	Irina	near "window"..... Cushioned, armless	Pull	Mike	In Reh.	x
11	3	F07	Chaise	Masha	Use from stock- will need slipcover/s, reinforce legs	Pull	Sandy	Upholstery	
12	3	F09	Chair		to use in grouping with chaise - "easy" chair variety.-JC Penny chairs	Pull	Mike	In Reh.	x
13	3	F11	Side table		Tea table, in grouping with chair and chaise	Pull	Meredith	In Reh.	x
14	3	F13	Cabinet/sidetable		Small, used as "bar", must hold liquor bottles concealed	Pull	Meredith	In Reh.	x
15	3	F14	Dining room table		to seat ten "cosy"	Build	Mike	New top	
16	3	F15-F16	Chairs		for ends of Dining room table- not part of "set"	Pull	Ann	Upholstery	
17	3	F17- F24	Dining room chairs		Matching 8	Pull	Ann	Upholstery	
18		F25	Chair		In LR - by F13- "matches" desk chair- can be used for party gathering at table	Pull	Ann	Upholstery	
19		F26	Chair		in LR - by stairway- "matches" desk chair- can be used for party gathering at table	Pull	Ann	Upholstery	
20	3	F30	Stone bench		In DR - will have "slipcover" to look like interior furniture until Act IV	Pull	Sandy	Paint	
21	3	F32-F33	Screens		In DR - Upstage dressed-Upholstery is two sided	Build	Mike/Ann	Paint	
22					**DRESSING/PRESET ITEMS ACT I**				
23	3	D01	Desk dressing		several books (5), possibly unlit candle	Pull	Meredith		X
24	3	D02	Sideboard dressing		Tray, 4 tulip shot glasses, red patterned runner	Pull	Meredith		x
25	3	D03	Sidetable		~~Lamp~~, picture of Icon	Buy/Build	Mike		
26		D03a	Picture of Icon		on D03	Research/Buld	Mike		
27	3	D04	Chaise dressing		2 Pillows and a beautiful throw on F07	Pull/Buy	Sandy		
28					**HAND PROPS ACT I**				
29	3	1101	Plates	Anfisa	Used to set table (Masha bangs w. fork on pg 17) May be brought in several "trips" to total 13	Pull	All		x
30		1102	Shoulder/hand towel	Anifsa	used throughout show	Pull	All		x
31	~~3~~	~~1104~~	~~Wine glasses~~	~~Anfisa~~	~~Used to set table - May be brought in several "trips" to total 13- may be cut~~	~~Buy~~			
32	~~3~~	~~1106~~	~~Water glasses~~	~~Anfisa~~	~~Used to set table (used by Fyodor on pag 17 to clink) May be brought in several "trips" to total 13~~	~~Buy~~			
33	3	1108	Silverware	Anfisa	Used to set table (Spoon used by Fyodor on pg 17 to clink glass -fork used by Masha on pg 17 to bang plate) May be brought in several "trips" to total 13	Pull	All		x
34	3	1110	Napkins	Anfisa	Used to set table May be brought in several "trips" to total 13	Pull			x
35	3	1116	Floral arrangement	Anfisa	Used to set table-white lillies	Build	Sandy		x
36	3	1120	Tray	Anfisa	1: wooden-Brings silverware, napkins, caviar 2: plates 3: chafing dishes To remove as necessary	Pull	All	IR	X
37	~~3~~	~~1126~~	~~Clock~~	~~on bar~~	~~"strikes" the hour~~				
38	3	1128	Book	Masha	"poetry" - read from	Pull	All	IR	X
39	~~4~~	~~1130~~	~~Paperwork~~	~~Olga~~	~~in a "messenger bag" (Costumes)~~				
40		1132	House Ledger	Olga	in a "messenger bag" (Costumes)	Pull	All	IR	X
41		1133	Grading book	Olga	carried- writings in	Pull	All	IR	X
42		1135	Small notebook	Olga	Tucked into belt/waistband	Pull	All	IR	X
43	5	1136	Violin w. bow	Andrey	Heard playing offstage- enters later on page 11	Pull/repair	Mike	IR	X
44	5	1140	Newspaper	Chebutkin	Read, also read on page 24, 51	Build	Mike	Research	
45	6	1144	Little bottle of cologne	Solyony	opened and rubbed on hands, from pocket - also used on page 31, 41, 54	Pull	All	IR	X
46	6	1148	Birthday cake	Ferapont	gift from Protopopov at the council Office- for Irina	Build	Meredith		
47		1149	Box for cake	Fearpont	Approx 18"x24", 4" high, cut out handles	Build	Meredith		
48	9	1150	Cards	The Baron	to play with Chebutkin	Pull	All	IR	X
49	13	1152	"Lunch"	Anfisa	"served" to all-2 silver covered dishes	Pull	All	IR	X
50	13	1168	Deacnter of vodka	Chebutkin	pours drinks for himself and Masha-on side board	Pull	All	IR	X
51	13	1170	Glasses	Chebutkin	pours drinks for himself and Masha	Pull	All	IR	X

FIGURE 1 Sample prop list used for *Three Sisters* showing all column listing and information. Courtesy of Meredith L. Roat, Properties Master, University of Wisconsin–Milwaukee.

director some leeway in reassigning duties or motivating the process. The prop list is often "updated" in this way at the beginning of the week in an informal meeting with the artisans to set weekly goals and sort through any problems in the process.

USING A TRACKING NUMBERS SYSTEM

The tracking number can be done in several ways, but a method easy to understand and implement is to use a four digit number with the first digit standing for the Act number, the second for the Scene number, and the last two for the prop number. Hence, the first prop listed in Act 1, Scene 3 would be 1301. If it had been in Act II, Scene 1, then it would have been 2101. Having more than 99 props in a given scene would be extraordinary so the system works. By simply looking at the prop number, you can tell when the prop is introduced onstage.

Props are given a number the *first* time they are used in the play. If a prop repeats, it may be listed in the particular scene listing by stage management tracking the prop, but it will track with its original number. Most working prop lists only list the prop the first time it is mentioned. Stage managers use the listings when they wish to track all the props in a scene and, therefore, may have props using all the different act numbers even in the final scene of the play.

The numbering system also allows an understanding of what works with what. For example, if you had a suitcase brought in during Act I, Scene 2, and was the sixth item added in that scene, its number would be 1206. This information is placed in the prop list along with the item name and whatever information is available. The listing for the suitcase might look like this:

> **1206 Suitcase Hard sided, brown, with leather straps, 22" tall, 30" wide, 8" deep**

If that suitcase was then opened in Act II, Scene 4 and had some items of clothing placed into the suitcase, that "dressing" would get its own number and it should have a notation to connect it to the right suitcase so that the props people know *which* suitcase gets the clothing. On the prop list as it is seen for the first time in Act II, Scene 4, it would look like this:

2401 Suitcase Dressing Placed in 1206, male clothing

This kind of detail becomes critical when a request comes in for the suitcase in Act I to be stood on by the actors and it is fitted for an interior brace needing to be removed during the scene change and clothing added. Then the listing would be:

1206 Suitcase Removable interior bracing to allow for actor to stand on it. Hard sided, brown, with leather straps, 22" tall, 30" wide, 8" deep

Or if the switch can't be made, then the suitcase has to be duplicated with an identical one for Act II.

2402 Suitcase Identical in appearance to 1206, dressed with 2401

The suitcase dressing should have its own number because it may require specific information to track with it, such as whether it is male or female, has some particular look or color to it. If something particular is requested, such as a pair of red high heel shoes to be thrown after being taken from the suitcase and are to be included as part of the dressing, then those red shoes should get assigned their own number as follows:

2403 Red Shoes Placed with 2401 in 2402, female, high heeled pumps, thrown (action)

It's helpful to leave spaces between assigned numbers when making up the prop list in anticipation of props being added. It's also acceptable to simply list the props in order of their being "added" and assign any additional added props the next number regardless of their relationship to another prop. The numbering system allows connections to be made regardless of either method used.

Assigning a numbering system to furniture and set dressing is helpful especially when tracking items in a multiple set show. Some lists use a listing simply by "place" utilizing an abbreviation to notate the location and then a number for tracking.

In a scene placed in a kitchen rotating with a scene in a bedroom, the prop list might look like this with K (kitchen) or B (bedroom), F (furniture), and D (dressing):

K F 1	Table	painted, seats four
K F 2	Chairs	4 identical, painted, matches K1
K F 4	Refrigerator	1950s, white, 32" wide
K D 1	Clock	Cat clock, tail wags, red
K D 2	Curtains	Spring rod in doorway, floor length, floral
B F 1	Bed	Twin bed mattress and box spring, jumped on
B F 2	Headboard	Painted black, goes with B1, must be strong
B F 3	Side table	Wooden, 20" tall, one shelf, one drawer
B D 2	Curtains	Spring rod in doorway, solid blue

Several props of the same item may each have their own independent numbers. For example, the four chairs described above could be KF 2, 3, 4, and 5 or could use subheadings like KF 2-a, b, c, and d to designate they are part of a group but have a separate identity number. This is especially helpful when tracking maintenance required on matching pieces and members of a group. If the show report says KF2-c is broken, the prop shop will know which chair they are talking about by referring to the storage list for postshow strike and can easily access the right chair without having to examine all the chairs.

On a unit set, the items can be simply listed as F (for furniture) or D (for dressing) with a number for tracking following it.

F 1	Chair	Side chair, upholstered, turned legs
F 2	Table	36" long, wooden, will be stood upon
D 1	Chandelier	Black metal, three arms, hangs center

Some lists break the numbering down similar to the hand props with coordination between Act and Scene using the F or D simply before the number. The ultimate goal is to do whatever works most easily and allows an organized build coordinating all the props.

Some prop shops do not utilize a numbering system because the builds are small or do not require this level of organization. *Do what works for you.* If the numbering system helps, work with stage management to make it a useful organizational and communication tool. Decide how you will assign numbers and communicate the information making it part of the rehearsal notes and tracking system for prop run. This is simply another tool to bring clarity and organization to the list.

GETTING STARTED

From the prop list, the properties director plans what might be built, pulled from stock and possibly modified, borrowed from another theatre or from a store, or bought in whole or in part. Part of this process is the consideration of what has to happen to complete each prop. Armed with whatever information available, the properties director must ask the following questions:

- What does it want to look like?
- What does it look like now?
- What does it need to do? (satisfying script/actor function/designer look/other production area interaction)
- How much/many are needed?
- Who handles it or makes it work?
- When does it need to be done?
- What talent is available to do it?
- What materials are available or can be obtained in the time allotted?
- What can be negotiated to change?
- How much money is it going to cost?
- How much time will it take to do it?

Not all these questions can be answered at first review and input from artisans on materials or time estimates may be needed. The properties director needs to make a "best guess" on what will work to begin the process of building or finding all the props.

Often, the list is broken down into *process lists*. A process list is a division of the prop list into the individual way the prop may be completed—built, borrowed, pulled, or bought. As the build progresses and choices get made, the viability of those options change and the process lists change.

For example, to build a table for the show, the buy list must reflect the materials needed such as wood, fasteners, specialty router bits, finishing stains, etc. But if a table is found in the stock of a furniture company willing to rent or lend it out, then all the lists change. The builder no longer has to build the table and the shopper no longer needs to buy materials, but must instead arrange for the transportation of the table. Or, the designer might find a table in stock that would work, but he wants a tablecloth made to disguise the top. This takes it off the build list for the carpenter artisan, but the buy list gets fabric and trim added to it and the soft goods artisan gets the fabric and trim to build the table covering.

This is where the mighty juggle against the budget of time and personnel begins, and the consummate skill of the properties director is needed most. The closer to tech and opening, the more complicated the juggle becomes.

Keeping the prop list up to date is mandatory, and communicating between all the involved partners any changes that occur is essential. Utilizing the prop list to coordinate the show build is covered in more depth in following chapters. The prop list is only one part of the information the properties director maintains. The prop list is informed by all the drawings, photographs, research, fabric samples, sketches, director/designer discussions, and other information communicated during the initial design and production coordination process.

SHOW BIBLE

To keep track of all the information, the properties director often gathers all the information from the preliminary design and production meetings and creates either a notebook or a computer file for all the changes occurring during the building process. This file or "show bible," as some call it, keeps all the show information in one place for easy reference.

Information to Include in Show Bible

Contact information sheet—phone, fax, email, and address
Production calendar—load-in, tech, and open
    Designer deadlines
    Rehearsal schedule
    Performance schedule
Weekly work/build schedule
Communication/email: (to and from)—designers, director, stage management, and all other production areas
Prop list
Rehearsal reports
Production meeting reports
Floor plans
Elevations
Designer drawings
Shop/working drawings
Research documentation/photos/sketches
Budget sheets
Copies of borrowing forms relevant to show use
Run crew list
Cast list
Program listing information/tracking
    Prop personnel—how they want to be listed, bios
    Acknowledgments
    Special thanks
Performance reports
Maintenance notes
Strike plan

As laptop computers, handheld tablets, and cell phones become standard management tools, the "bible" is transitioning into a digital resource with images scanned in and calendars, budgets, rehearsal reports, prop lists, and such all being kept in accessible files and available electronically. Because most of this information is now being communicated via the computer, keeping it as an electronic file makes sense. Having this information available electronically is especially helpful if available from "the cloud" or similar accessible online method of storing it. It is easy to update and track changes on the computer and send responses to stage management, the production manager, or other production shops via email, especially helpful when responding to rehearsal reports so everyone is part of the conversation. Using it as the basis for managing the build, all information is readily available in meetings attended, while shopping with the designer, for an artisan who has questions, to track communications between the shop and rehearsal, to review drawings for specific information, and to resolve any questions that might arise. Receipts can be scanned in allowing originals to be processed to bookkeeping as necessary. Artisans can access the information easily and print off copies or download the information to their personal electronic devices, study the designer's notes or research, and read rehearsal report comments about how a prop is used to clarify their thought process as they work on the show.

This information can be printed off as necessary, saving paper and keeping the information safe and in a format that is easily updated. The three-ring binder "bible" is quickly becoming a relic of the past. If the information is hard copied and kept in a physical notebook, the juggle of keeping the information secure is somewhat more difficult. When an artisan needs a drawing or other information, they should make one for their use, but the original stays with the notebook so there is always a single source for all the information.

If electronic files are unavailable or the theatre does not utilize smart phones/ipads, etc., then the shopper may have a similar folder-based "bible" to use while searching for the pieces needing to be bought or for information on items needing specific lengths or sizes of materials. This should duplicate the information kept in the shop bible, but the properties director's "bible" stays in the shop, insuring its security and available for use by the in-house staff.

Usually, the properties director manages the shop bible (electronic or otherwise), and all changes are tracked and noted so the information is up to date creating a single source for all questions. Regardless of how the information is stored, the shop bible is a critically important organizational and management tool for the build on any show.

Chapter 5

Budgeting

Following initial design meetings with the scenic designer and the director to talk through the preliminary hand prop list and study the elevations or scale model for all the set props and dressing, the properties director now has a listing and the information of what is wanted. The big question is "Can we afford it?" To answer that question, a preliminary show budget must be created. The *preliminary show budget* estimates the cost of materials for items having to be built, modified, and purchased as well as the labor estimate for the build. Each item on the prop list should have a cost associated with it, given the preliminary supposition of how it might be completed. Every properties director knows that this preliminary budget is, at best, a wildly optimistic (or pessimistic) best guess. The juggle done in the prop shop on how any one show gets built can be completed in a multitude of ways depending on what stroke of fortune allows the right fabric to be found for pennies on the dollar, what furniture can be borrowed or found in stock, and how accurate the prop list remains to the first listing. Making a preliminary show budget is oftentimes an exercise in futility but, frankly, it should be done as a means to begin defining the show and what it will take to build it as designed. Without one, all too often what was once considered scenery or a costume can magically become props based on cost overruns in the areas with more preliminary information in the design process.

With a budget based on what props are known at the time and a healthy contingency fund to cover the "what ifs," it is possible to give the production manager an assessment of the expected budget impact and be able to negotiate changes based on anticipated expenses and build times.

Often the properties director will request information from the properties artisans who will be completing the work on a specific project or prop. Chairs needing upholstery should be measured and yardage figured. Furniture to be built must have board feet estimated. Any prop being built or modified can, on some basic level, be broken down into a materials budget. Completing a written estimate helps keep the projections organized. A simple materials breakdown might look something like this:

Materials Estimate Build of Furniture Piece

By Props Carpenter to Props Director

Item	Description	Cost ($)
Lumber	Plywood and poplar 5/4 stock	229.00
	Interior bracing-pine 1 × 12	22.00
Hardware	Hinges-Strap, brass 18"	7.50
	Swivel casters-4	38.50
Finish	Stain-Mahogany	12.00
	Satin varnish	18.50
Misc. Supplies	Sandpaper, shop rags	7.00
Total		334.50

Finishing supplies such as paint, trim, molding, hardware, etc. not available in stock should have quantity estimated and priced. Items being modified from stock should account for whatever needs to be purchased to complete the modification. Items having to be found and purchased should be researched online or in stores for availability and pricing. Allowances for shipping expenses should be included in the budget. Rental payments, when purchasing is not an option, might also be a factor in the budget estimate. When a show is set in a particular style or period, an allowance should be built into the budget acknowledging the difficulty of reproducing or purchasing items to fit that style. In addition, in each budget, a contingency of at least 20% is often added to account for the additions, changes, and cuts occurring during the process of production.

Before rehearsal, the prop list is only a rough guideline and it will change throughout the rehearsal process, sometimes impacting a budget severely. As a properties director becomes familiar with designers and directors, this contingency figure may need to increase or might be decreased based on those prior production experiences. Some directors and designers are less able to think through all of the script needs until the production parts are assembled and onstage. All too often, props is the area called upon to "fix" whatever difficulty is created whether it's adding foliage to cover a bad seam where scenery comes together, adding more dressing to disguise a sight line, or finding a different piece of furniture due to an unforeseen shift problem. Contingency figures also help cover when the cost of materials fluctuate. For example, plywood often increases in price and availability during a severe hurricane season.

Reviewing the prop list, it is easy to run down the list assigning a cost to each prop based on a preliminary judgment of how it will be completed. Once costs are projected for each prop, a preliminary prop materials budget can be completed and submitted to the production manager. It is important to remind the production and design team that *props is a constantly evolving area*. The changes during the staging and rehearsal process usually require continual reevaluation of budget and priorities. Compromise and negotiation of fiscal priorities will be ongoing as the build moves closer to technical rehearsals. The collaborative process with the designer is all important in making decisions utilizing the best choices in spending the money wisely over the entire build and enabling the props to have an equity in completion. Props added at the last minute must be considerate of the money remaining to buy the item or the materials needed to build the item, as well as the labor available to complete the addition.

A second budget should accompany the materials budget estimating the personnel labor: the hours available and/or needed for the build. One labor hour is one person working for 1 hour.

Labor estimates serve two purposes beyond just informing administration of the anticipated time allowance needed. First, they allow the artisan to break down the project into specific process steps determining the

products needed to accomplish the work, honing a specific plan for building. Second, examination of the process allows discovery of other options
available to save time or money. Although a useful tool, this is often only
done in the case where a number of large projects need to be juggled for
priority in the build or where the properties director needs to negotiate
with the designer regarding other options or alternative solutions.

Other considerations in the labor budget might include the need for
estimating additional outside labor to be hired in on a project larger than
the full-time staff can accomplish or on a project requiring specialized
skills. Just as in the materials budget, a contingency should be allotted
to give some leeway in the estimate allowing for sick days, difficulties
with a project, or changes coming from rehearsal forcing a change in the
design and build of a prop.

Creating a labor estimate and showing budget require a broad understanding of the processes required to fulfill the production of properties.
An analysis of the prop list and all the possible ways it can be "solved"

Labor Estimate

From Soft Goods Artisan to Properties Director

Chair Upholstery	Project Process Hours
Fabric preparation—wash/dye/distress	4 hours (processing time)
Chair stripping	4 hours
Chair structural or finish repairs, modifications	6–12 hours (dry time necessary)
Padding restoration/layering	3 hours
Patterning/draping and layout	6 hours
Muslin re-cover	2.5 hours
Final fabric cover	3.5 hours
Trim	1 hour
Total	30–36 *hours*

Note: Other projects can be worked on intermittently during dye processing and glue/
stain/dry times.

almost make this a "best guess" scenario. Although scenery may be able to budget labor based on the normal and usual process of building stock units of platforms or walls, it is a rare thing in props to duplicate a process is a similar fashion. With experience and hands-on practice, it is possible to make a guesstimate about what might be a reasonable expectation for labor to accomplish some specific task such as to reupholster a chair or to build a table. But, of course, every estimate is impacted by the variables of the skill/experience of the person doing the work, the availability of materials, the difficulty of the final "look," and what other things also need to be accomplished in the same space by the same worker. Each build and each designer demand a level of specificity making prior labor timelines moot in most cases. That said, it's helpful to make a guesstimate even if it's only to help in the prioritization of project work and to assist the shopper in knowing what supplies need to be in the shop by what date. It helps in the process of defining whether the "work load" is possible during any given build and assists the properties director in creating a calendar and deadline schedule. It also gives a perspective on how to make some of the decisions cropping up in every build. Some things can be negotiated but others not.

The preliminary materials and labor budgets are shared with the production manager and designer for any negotiation in design changes required to bring the show in on budget and completed by opening. At this point, the negotiation between departments might occur, with another department either offering to pay for part of a project materials expense if the work is completed by the prop shop, by sharing labor resources interdepartmentally, or agreeing to take on the entire project as part of the other departments load. In extreme cases, it may mean the designer making substantive changes to the design or the production manager using contingency funding to help cover some of the budget overage or to hire in extra workers. Knowing the potential costs at the start of the build helps everyone to make better choices.

SPREADSHEET TRACKING

As the build begins, all purchases are tracked in the *show budget*. Working closely with the shopper, the properties director keeps a spreadsheet allowing the expenses on a show to be monitored and anticipated.

As purchases are completed and estimates become reality, the budget is juggled allowing choices to be made with an understanding of the overall impact each decision creates. For example, the designer may be given a choice between prioritizing one project over another. Buy the $40 a yard fabric for the chairs and use a table in stock or buy $15 a yard fabric for the chairs and buy a new table, or lumber to build a table matching the design better than the stock table. Each choice is correct depending on what resources are available and creates the strongest image of support for the play. Each choice costs in different way, one more labor intensive and the other weighted toward purchased items. The management of financial resources or priorities and what is best for the design is a constant juggle requiring close collaboration between the shop and design team.

The *budget spreadsheet* can be a simple accounting of what has been purchased, or one can divide it by project and identify purchases specific to each project. The value of itemizing each item purchased against a specific prop allows the final cost expense to be determined at the end of the build. It's also handy to have a method of tracking what has been spent on specific projects to assist in future budget projections, but often the data entry of information is problematic and time consuming. Some properties directors have the prop shopper, if they have one, enter this information in the spreadsheet. As a management tool, a budget spreadsheet can be as complex as time allows creating a searchable database for many purposes.

Most shows require only a simple spreadsheet showing what has been purchased, from whom it was purchased, what it cost, when it was purchased, and how it was purchased. A simple description might be added to help jog the memory of what it was used for or to notate a specific amount or other potentially important information. This is particularly helpful when, in the future, it's necessary to track down where you bought something because it's needed again, and all that can be remembered is it was bought for a particular show. Go to the budget, scroll down through the items purchased, and the information is there—job done!

Setting up a standard spreadsheet and working with the shopper to be sure all invoices and receipts are entered on a timely basis allows the properties director to keep current on what has been spent and allows decisions on anticipated buying to be relevant to the remaining budget.

	THREE SISTERS		SHOW BUDGET			
Date	Vendor	Item	Description	Cost	How	2,500
22.2.12	PayPal	Tray	antique hammered brass samovar tray	$50.00	Visa	$2,450
26.2.12	PayPal, ThinkFastToys	Top	spinning/humming	$13.04	Visa	$2,436.96
23.2.12	American Science and Surplus	Bottle, cork	cologne?	$0.48	PC	$2,436.48
1.3.12	World Market	Misc	Bunny, tumblers, frame, 18" toss pillow	$62.94	Visa	$2,373.54
3.3.12	PayPal,	Kerosene Lamp	Antique 1880 German Kerosene Oil Lamp	$76.19	Visa	
3.3.12	Michaels	Flowers	false flora	$14.79	Visa	
3.3.12	Menards	Stove materials	carved rubber, crib, canopy kit, 6" finishing	$23.93	Visa	$2,349.61
6.3.12	PayPal	Clock	Vintage Holland Electric mantle	$41.00	Visa	$2,308.61
11.3.12	Target	Bathroom	waste basket, pitcher and washbowl	$60.97	Visa	$2,247.64
13.3.12	Furniturebuy.com	Desk	Pulaski Accents Paulette Desk	$438.90	Visa	
13.3.12	Menards	for Heater	misc. parts	$52.51	Visa	$1,756.23
14.3.12	Home Depot	Lumber	for chairs, desk, and screen frames.	$223.93	Visa	$1,532.30
19.3.12	Furniturebuy.com	Desk	Pulaski Accents Desk - BACKORDERED	$438.90	REFUND	$1,971.20
21.3.12	Etsy: TomsBarn	Camera	Hand prop	$37.50	Visa	$1,933.70
22.3.12	Vogue Fabrics	Fabric	Grey, possible chaise slipcover	$35.91	Visa	$1,897.79
24.3.12	PayPal, Western Bid, Inc	Cup Holders	Russian Samovar glass holders	$62.98	Visa	$1,834.81
26.3.12	Bazaar	Fabric	for bench and chairs	$329.81	Visa	
26.3.12	Calico Corners	Fabric	for screen sides-act I	$107.93	Visa	
26.3.12	Jo-Ann Fabric	Fabric	for screen sides-act II	$58.54	Visa	$1,338.53
26.3.12	Paper Mart	Tissue paper	for leaves	$81.87	Visa	$1,256.66
7.3.12	PayPal, Overstock.com	Goblets	Wine glasses, champagne flutes: crystal	$124.63	Visa	$1,132.03
27.3.12	World Market	Glasses	shot type, for vodka	$41.85	Visa	$1,090.18
28.3.12	Utrecht	Various art.	Newsprint, B&J cleaner	$28.49	Visa	
28.3.12	Broadway Paper	Paper	Packaging (for tea box) and tissue/wrap	$58.13	Visa	$1,003.56
29.3.23	World Market	Bottles, glasses	For perfume/cologne, for vodka	$21.67	Visa	
29.3.23	TJ Maxx	Home items	Kitchen item, stationary, domestics	$29.54	Visa	
29.3.23	Jo-Ann Fabric	Trimp	For footstool, JC Penny chairs, etc	$75.28	Visa	$877.07
31.3.12	Elliot Ace Hardware	Various	cabinet lock, epoxy, barge cement, glaze,	$87.42	Visa	$789.65
2.4.12	Jo-Ann Fabric	Stencils	For screen painting	$114.91	Visa	
2.4.12	Jo-Ann Fabric	Toweling	For bedroom	$41.68	Visa	$633.06
4.4.12	Chattel Changers	Kitchen	adornments	$50.68	Visa	
4.4.12	Menards	Hardware	glides, hinges	$18.25	PC	$564.13
5.4.12	Hahn Ace Hardware	Various	Lamp supplies, tape, water putty	$38.43	Visa	
5.4.12	The Paint Shop	Paint	faux wood	$32.35	Visa	$493.35
9.4.12	Jo-Ann Fabric	Trims	ribbon, gimp	$19.16	Visa	$474.19
10.4.12	Home Depot	Hardware	hinges, corner braces, felt pad	$31.50	Visa	$442.69
12.4.12	Jo-Ann Fabric	Fabric	for x-backed chairs	$43.33	Visa	
12.4.12	Target	Various	candy', tape, crayons	$27.47	Visa	$371.89
13.4.12	Precious Ceramics	Clocks	cast and fired	$96.00	PC	$275.89
14.4.12	Menards	Liquid nails	stove "iron" attachment	$29.56	Visa	$246.33
18.4.12	Menards	Cake supplies	Silicone caulk, power grab	$23.16	Visa	
18.4.12	Walmart	Glasses	for samovar cup holders	$24.67	Visa	$198.50
19.4.12	Utrecht	Paint	for screens	29.64	Visa	$168.86
20.4.12	Winkie's	Misc.	Wrapping paper	13.66	Visa	
20.4.12	Winkie's	cardboard	for screens	6.33	Visa	$148.87
24.4.12	FleetFarm	Lamp	chimney for kerosene lamp	5.06	Visa	$143.81
25.4.12	Jo-Ann Fabric	Pen	Gold leaf pen for screens	7.14	Visa	$136.67
29.4.12	Pick'n'Save	Cs	olives, peanuts, instant tea, bread	34.95	Visa	$101.72
29.4.12	PayPal, Overstock.com	glasses	backups	52.50	Visa	$49.22
					FINAL:	$49.22

FIGURE 1 Show budget tracking of all purchases made for the prop work on the show. Note it is "searchable" by any of the headers allowing information to be found quickly and to see an overview of the decisions made as the show progressed. Courtesy of Meredith L. Roat, Properties Master, University of Wisconsin–Milwaukee.

It is helpful to track *how* supplies were purchased especially in the event items need to be returned or if a problem occurs with the item. Most theatres use a credit card for the majority of their purchases, and the credit card companies will assist with problems when items are purchased using their credit card. In addition, the credit cards can be coded specific to a shop and used for all purchases in that area. Some shops have multiple cards allowing each card to be specific to a budget line such as show budget, overhead, vehicle, etc. or to allow more than one person to be shopping. Some theatres still work with purchase orders or have accounts set up with particular vendors. Finally, cash transactions are utilized in some instances.

If using petty cash, it is crucial all receipts are safeguarded until recorded and submitted for reimbursement, otherwise you're just out of the money. Most theatres use a standard reporting form to itemize purchases made with petty cash, and the receipts are submitted along with an accounting of what budget to charge against. In some organizations, the prop shop is advanced a set amount of petty cash at the start of the season to accommodate the purchasing requiring the use of cash such as flea markets, individuals, and small businesses when either the vendor is unable to accept a credit card or the amount of the purchase is too small. By submitting receipts, the petty cash advance is replenished as the season progresses, and the advance is turned in at the end of the season by either reimbursing the amount as cash or as a combination of cash and receipts.

KINDS OF BUDGETS

In addition to the show budget, the properties director often has several other budget lines to manage. Size of organization and kind of administrative structure will determine who controls what budget and how they are reported.

The *overhead* budget (sometimes called supplies or shop perishables budget) is used to purchase bulk supplies for an *entire season* of shows. This allows better pricing on materials and keeps the shop supplied, so work is not dependent on the arrival of materials purchased on an "as-needed" basis. The items often purchased on the overhead budget may include muslin, foam rubber, upholstery batting, sewing sundries, staples, sandpaper, hardware (nuts, bolts, nails, angle irons, pop rivets, casters, etc.), brown paper for layout, glues, white and black paint, spray paints, tints, brushes, sealers, latex gloves, dust masks, hearing protection, office supplies, etc. The overhead budget purchases those consumable items used in the building of props over the entire season and cannot be easily attributed to a single show.

A tool and shop *maintenance* budget is often utilized to buy new tools or to fix/replace broken tools. This budget purchases those items used over *multiple seasons* and builds. Items purchased on this type of budget often include ladders, rolling carts, storage units, computers, software upgrades, new tools, etc.

Some organizations keep this budget at the production management level or even higher administratively in a facilities budget viewing these expenses as a capitol improvement. In that case, the properties director must work to ensure administration understands the importance of providing funding for replacement and maintenance of shop tools as an immediate need while planning for future improvements and anticipated larger item replacements. Depending on the accessibility and openness of the relationship between production and administration (usually a reflection of the size of the organization), this structure of control over the budget and how it gets spent may work as easily as having a designated prop budget for tool maintenance.

Some development departments have undertaken specific fundraising events to support the renovation of production spaces and the upgrading of equipment or sought out donors having a special interest in the production side of theatre to underwrite the purchase of a special tool outside usual budget considerations. Similarly, the marketing department will sometimes offer show tickets or advertising in the program in exchange for materials and services necessary to production. Getting the folks in these offices to understand and appreciate how their support of the production areas generally benefits the bottom line will open the door to all sorts of ways to support the theatre and the shops.

Most regional theatres have the support of the theatre administration, backed by the marketing and development offices, to budget for large ticket items and shop renovations at the "facilities" level, balanced with a tool and maintenance "seasonal" budget managed by the properties director to keep tools maintained for safe operation and replace small ticket items on an as-needed basis.

Some organizations have a single budget line for both overhead and tool/shop maintenance. It is handy to have the budgets split, even if only internally, to enable the properties director to see what is used in show production versus the overall production costs for tools and shop maintenance. This understanding is especially helpful when working with estimating budgets in collaboration with the production manager. It is important to track how the *overhead* budget is spent because a single show can consume more than it's fair share of the supplies bought to cover the season. Understanding the support the overhead budget gave to a particular show can illuminate budget planning for upcoming seasons having similar shows. Higher budget adjustments should be made to compensate for the additional expenses the overhead budget covered.

Some theatres may require the properties director to manage budgets for vehicle/travel, prop storage facility rental, and over-hire personnel.

The *vehicle/travel* budget often covers the maintenance of a company vehicle, personal reimbursement of mileage when a member of the prop shop uses their own car for business use such as prop shopping or moving items from prop storage to the theatre, expenses for rental vehicles, gas and tolls, and/or parking expenses. Some organizations use this budget to cover travel for the properties staff when attending conferences or when it is necessary for a properties staff member to travel to another city when working on a co-production or for design meetings. In those cases, keeping in touch with administration to ensure adequate funding has been set aside is important.

A prop *storage* budget may account for any expenses associated with where the props are stored including monthly rental fees, heating or cooling, purchasing of carts and moving equipment, and any space maintenance issues. This budget might also be just a smaller budget to cover things like light bulbs, cleaning supplies, and moving equipment and materials (i.e., boxes, moving pads, carts), and the actual rental or facility upkeep is covered at the administrative level. It is tracked separately from the overhead or shop tools/maintenance budget to track expenses related specifically to the props storage areas.

Another area usually maintained by upper theatre administration (i.e., managing director or production manager) is *personnel* hiring even when it is an over-hire situation including hiring, payment, taxes, and withholding. However, the prop shop will need to track hours and time used from their allotted budget of money. Those prop shops utilizing over-hire personnel may have a variety of folks hired as specialty artists or to assist when a load-in or strike requires extra hands. Depending on skill level and how long the person has worked at the theatre, pay will vary. Determining who is hired and how much they are paid is often left to the discretion of the properties director. The properties director contacts the potential over-hire artisan and then processes time sheets or a weekly reporting of hours to administration, allowing an accurate tracking of people hired and money remaining in the over-hire budget. As with any budget, the properties director should occasionally confirm the accuracy of those figures to ensure the shop figures are in agreement with administration and to alert upper management if a deficit seems likely.

Those organizations renting out their prop stock or selling their stock may also need to have a separate budget line tracking the *income* so it can be turned in to the theatre or used for a special project. Other theatre companies simply put the money into their overhead or maintenance budgets indicating it as an "income" line item.

BOOKKEEPING AND REPORTING

The level of bookkeeping and reporting often is reflective of the size of the organization and the level of accountability to the various administrative units over the production area. What some theatres see as an administrative budget, others would prefer to simply assign funds and allow the prop shop to manage their money for the season reporting in as necessary or by some set schedule. Generally, the show budgets are reported to the production manager, whereas the other budgets reflecting entire seasonal expenditures are reported to either the production manager or the managing director. The properties director may get reports from central bookkeeping of the theatre to justify accounts on a monthly or seasonal basis. Some organizations use online reporting systems to track all purchasing allowing the production manager to have an up-to-the-minute view of where the budget is on any given show or account. Entering the information so the account is up to date can be part of the shopper's job or may fall under the responsibilities of the properties director.

Accurate reporting is critical and those who manage and allot the company finances appreciate budget control. When sound financial management is demonstrated in the prop shop, administration can trust the estimates and decisions made knowing the money is well spent to the benefit of the show and the theatre itself.

Chapter 6

The Rehearsal and Production Process

Properties production is the one area in technical production relying most highly on getting information directly from the day-to-day rehearsal process. During rehearsal, hand props not mentioned in the script get added, furniture is used in a specific way impacting how it should be built or reinforced, a prop gets thrown and broken each night as part of the new staging making it a consumable item or an actor is allergic to wool and needs a cotton blanket for the bed covering. This information cannot come from the designer, the script, or research. It is directly learned from the rehearsal process itself specific to this group of actors and this director. Information flow is critical as the play is staged when props are added, cut, use is changed, or stage action altered. Getting the information from rehearsal and open to discussion by all involved parties allows the prop department to build the props in support of what needs to happen for the show. This information is communicated in the daily rehearsal report.

THE REHEARSAL REPORT

Because prop people can't be everywhere, God made *stage managers*. They are our eyes in rehearsal and our advocates in the production process to directors, actors, and run crews.

The rehearsal report should include the following:

What part of the play was rehearsed, who was in attendance
Changes to calendar, rehearsal schedule or actor "calls"
Requests for upcoming rehearsals or meetings
Notification of meetings scheduled
Rehearsal notes listing by department:
- ■ Adds
- ■ Cuts
- ■ Changes in use
- ■ Maintenance issues
- ■ General information/questions

Stage managers generate the rehearsal reports following each rehearsal and forward them to all involved parties. *Rehearsal reports* contain the "who, what, where, when, why and how" of what's happening with the entire rehearsal and staging process, including props and all other technical areas.

In the area of props, it is especially important that stage managers communicate specific details having an impact on the prop choices. This might include timing factors such as the length of a candle burn time, actor allergies or preferences for consumables, special needs for weapons or special effects with the audience or the stage space, or difficulties anticipated for scene shifts due to actor availability, weight or size of items, or storage space backstage. It is of equal importance that stage managers define the situation or problem and not the solution when giving notes (e.g., "The actor needs to be able to sit on the stool with both feet on the floor and the stools are too tall" NOT "Please cut four inches off the stool legs.").

The director should approve all *rehearsal notes*. Notes from actors must be cleared through both the stage management and the director before they are put on the rehearsal report. Not only does this keep the director in the loop about any requests but also guarantees the notes accurately reflect the directorial viewpoint. Some actors make requests to the director that they would not want or need in the scene, and this "clearing" process keeps the communication free from any confusion.

The Importance of Being Earnest   Rehearsal report #11

Date: Monday, September 1
PSM: Anita Coffee
Absent/Late: None
Injuries: None

Schedule: Today - blocking of Act I and spacing onstage.
Wednesday – complete blocking of Act II/spacing
Friday – complete blocking of Act III/spacing

SCENERY:
1. Please confirm all furniture/dressing can ride on turntable in shift.
2. Can rugs be attached to offstage step units? Actors are concerned about tripping.

PROPS:
1. See Lights note #2, #3. ADD: light switch
2. CUT: Lane's butler book.
3. Tea set-up for top of act should be: Tray with teapot, hot water pot, sugar bowl w. cubed sugar w. tongs, and creamer. 2nd tray with three teacups and saucers, teaspoons, napkins, and side plates. Tiered tray with removable plates holding cucumber sandwiches and bread and butter sandwiches. Actors request NON-caffeine tea.
4. Actor requests thin cream cheese spread for cucumber sandwiches and asks for very thin slices of cucumber.
5. Please "garnish" bread and butter sandwich plate so total sandwiches is eight sandwiches. Actor prefers crust-less sandwiches and low fat butter of margarine.
6. ADD: Tray with additional tea cup/saucer, side plate, teaspoon, napkin. Servant brings in on page 5 following Jack's entry.
7. No cigarettes will be smoked...actor will open case and remove one but never actually lights one.
8. Lady Bracknells notebook comes from her purse.
9. Lane's bell button is on wall under light switch. No other "bell" is needed.
10. Sherry set should be: Tray with Sherry decanter and three footed sherry glasses. Actor requests cranberry juice for sherry.
11. Algernon will pick up railway guide to write address - he will NOT be writing on this shirt cuff. He will use a pen he takes from his pocket.
12. Jack will put the cigarette case in his pocket.

COSTUMES:
1. Lady Bracknells "pencil" for writing in notebook should be attached to a retractable chain hanging from a brooch or other jewelry piece.
2. See prop note #8, 10, 11.

LIGHTS:
1. Confirming footlights have some kind of protective cage/cover - how close can we get? Women have long dresses and the blocking places actors sitting on downstage "poul" and walking around it.
2. We would like to place the light switch for the chandeller somewhere near the fireplace entry.
3. Lamp on desk will be switched on by Lady Bracknell to write her notes.

SOUND:
1. Lane's bell from wall call button is "silent".

MISCELLANEOUS:
We will be having a stumble-through of all acts on Monday of next week. We would appreciate using cigarette case, notebook, and all writing materials in rehearsal if they are available.

FIGURE 1   Example of a rehearsal report for *The Importance of Being Earnest* showing the kind of detail and the importance of effective communication between the rehearsal space and the shops.

Rehearsal reports are emailed after each rehearsal to facilitate the best communication. The properties director reads the report, updates the prop list as necessary, and sends on additional information or design concerns to the scenic designer. Requests should be discussed with the designer and decisions made in collaborative discussion with the production areas. Some requests can be immediately answered and should be responded to by return email copying all concerned parties.

In the case of larger or more complex requests, the properties director prepares for the designer/director/cross-departmental concerns to be addressed in the next production meeting or might seek out information/assistance on a project by meeting separately with another department or colleague. Meanwhile in the prop shop, changes to projects in process will need to be discussed with the artisan in charge of the project and work may be redirected until answers can be provided affecting the project in question.

PRODUCTION MEETING

The *production meeting* is the venue where all areas can share information, clarify the needs of the departments, establish deadlines, and work on creating a schedule with consideration for each department's priorities. Generally led by the production manager, rehearsal notes and upcoming deadlines form the basis of most of the discussions occurring in the weekly production meetings. The *production manager* coordinates all production activities throughout the production season and leads the entire production team to a successful season of shows produced on-time, on-budget, and meeting the director and designer's vision.

The properties director should strive to have a strong working relationship with the production manager, ensuring good communication on issues involving calendar, budget, personnel, and design parameters. The properties director utilizes the production manager to resolve issues between the shops or when difficulties arise with a designer or director. A comfortable open relationship is valuable in making sure the prop shop has an equal voice as the production moves forward through the build/tech/run/strike process. When budgets get strained or designs inflated, the production manager is the person who should step in to sort things out, define priorities based on the overview of the show, and juggle personnel and budgets to match needs. The production manager is often the person who deals with facilities and company vehicle issues as well.

The properties director should attend all production meetings to keep everyone informed about the status of the properties build, to clarify any concerns from rehearsal, and to ask and answer questions about areas of production overlap necessitating collaboration. In props, overlap is common. Props are one of the most interconnected departments in the theatre production area. Sharing the load of production by splitting the labor or dividing up the materials cost of a project uses the strengths of all departments, allowing a better product through close production teamwork.

REHEARSAL PROPS

In many regional theatres, stage management has a stock storage closet of hand props and an assemblage of furniture pieces in the rehearsal hall to be accessed for use during the rehearsal process. *Rehearsal props* stand in for the actual prop as the actor works out the stage action and movement in the rehearsal process. Many theatres use an odd gathering of castoff furniture pieces to set the rehearsal space. Some use a cube system with standardized 18" wooden rehearsal cubes to represent the furniture complimented by assorted armchairs and other real items to complete the rehearsal kit. Stage managers should not expect the prop shop to provide rehearsal props but should use what they can best create or pull from their rehearsal stock on their own to stand-in for the actual item. But for specialty pieces not available in the stage management stock, the prop shop often works with the stage managers to assist in procuring something similar from prop storage to be used. An understanding of what the actual item looks like allows the stage manager to communicate accurate information to the actor and will inform their choices in selecting a rehearsal prop. A visit to the prop shop to see the actual prop or talking with the properties director about what a prop might look like and how it is to be used allows the stage manager to provide a more accurate representation in rehearsal.

FIGURE 2 Actors working in the rehearsal room using rehearsal furniture—
Hayfever, Kurt Sharp, Scenic Designer, University of Wisconsin–Milwaukee.

FIGURE 3 Actors on fully dressed set using the designed furniture—*Hayfever*,
Kurt Sharp, Scenic Designer, University of Wisconsin–Milwaukee.

It is helpful when the furniture used in rehearsal duplicates the qualities of the actual furniture piece. If a chair is to have arms or an especially high back, then the rehearsal piece should have some representation of that even if it is only a piece of cardboard taped to the sides to represent arms or the back of the chair showing a similar height as the real prop chair. This allows the actors to understand the relationship of their movement in and around the chair to the actual prop.

If the staging requires specific action difficult to duplicate with a rehearsal prop, stage management may request the use of the actual furniture piece for several rehearsals to establish the action with the actor. Most prop shops either provide the actual piece in rehearsal or a close duplicate serving both the rehearsal process and allowing an easier adjustment once the rehearsal moves to the stage and uses the actual chair. Some shop-built furniture pieces might be sent to rehearsal before final finishing for actors to get comfortable with the actual piece and then pulled for completion as the prop shop moves into the final weeks of the build.

Once scripts are out of the actor's hands, it is helpful to have something to represent the hand props the actors will be working with to help them hook the action to the language. During the exploratory time while actors are experimenting with how they are working a scene or playing around with ways to interact, using plastic or nonbreakable items allows the actors to work the scenes without fear of breaking props or hurting themselves on a piece of broken glass or china. It is important the actors move to either the actual prop or something duplicating the weight and feel of the actual prop once the scenes are set and the action defined to help the actors understand how the actual prop might work. If an actor is blocked to carry a tray with six glasses, it is best to know the size of the tray and if the glasses are footed champagnes or flat based "on the rocks" style glasses. For those problematic specialty props such as weapons or something manipulated in a specific way, often the prop shop will prioritize the completion of those props to allow them to move to rehearsal before technical rehearsals onstage. Actors who have been working with a facsimile in rehearsal that is significantly larger or heavier, or that opens in a different way than the actual prop, may have a more difficult time in the technical rehearsals when so many other changes (lights, sound, spacing, etc.) are also occurring and the prop usually comes out on the short end of that process.

COSTUMES

In many organizations, props will collaborate with costumes more than any other production area. Both props and costumes provide the items closest to the actor and, hence, are most connected to character. Costume designers use props to help complete a costume ensemble, and the items the character carries or uses must be considered and chosen to fit within the definition of the designed look. Some costume shops have a costume prop artisan to complete those costume items, but often the coordination of personal items needs a discussion between the costume designer and the properties director to determine style, color, size, and placement such as for a wallet, notebook, briefcase, or knife sheath. Working with the costume designer follows a similar research, option presentation, and response as with the scenic designer. The prop shop works to fulfill the look, defining the character as designed by the costume designer just as they work to fulfill the setting requirements as designed by the scenic designer. Often these discussions are a full collaborative discussion and decision-making process with both designers and shops involved.

Decisions about costume color palette and pattern might impact choices for props. Before shopping for upholstery, drapery, or other soft good fabrics, it is a good idea to know what the costumes look like. For costumes that are pulled or borrowed, the properties director can look at the items for each actor to inform the fabric selection process. For items being built, small fabric swatches can be cut for prop shop use. Coordinating the look between the shops is important to prevent a clash of color, pattern or texture, or having it look too similar, which can be equally disastrous.

Is it a prop or a costume? Generally speaking, if you wear it, then it is a costume; if you carry it, it is a prop. Each theater determines the answer, but most regional theatre costume shops have their own costume craft person who deals with these types of crossover requests in collaboration with the prop shop. For example, umbrellas (props) and parasols (costumes); flower bouquets (props) and boutonnieres (costumes); handbags (costume) and suitcase (props); eyeglasses (costume) and opera glasses (prop). This is not a hard and fast rule but a simple way to help figure out who is responsible for what and everything is certainly negoti-able. Sometimes one shop takes on a project that in other circumstances might be completed by the other shop. It often has to do with who has the time, the expertise, the budget, or the interest in doing the project.

The costume shop often comes to the prop shop for assistance on casting and molding projects or when needing to use tools not usually found in the costume shop. Projects requiring prosthetics, missing limbs, extra tall extensions of legs, or peg legs are good examples of situations where the prop shop often collaborates to create fake body parts, build or find stilts to be built into a costume, or layout and turn a peg leg on the props lathe. Props crafts people may also work on costume crafts objects such as crowns or jewelry items, when the costume shop lacks the skills, tools, or time to complete the job.

Masks and puppetry productions usually involve a close collaboration between the prop and costume shops. For large puppets or units involv-ing internal structuring, the costume shop often relies on the expertise of the prop shop for construction of the framework or armature, while they build the external costume. Many prop shops build the masks or collaborate with the crafts person in the costume shop, to complete the mask production. This may occur by dividing the process into definable processes, with the casting of the actors face done as a team project, the mask forms being built and painted in the prop shop, and the final decoration and fitting of the masks done by costumes.

Weaponry also presents a opportunity for costume/prop collabora-tion. The weapon is always a prop, but finding a way for the weapon to be carried or worn by the actor requires a close collaboration between the shops. Belts are a costume and a baldric or any sword carrier is usu-ally produced in the costume crafts shop so that it will look and hang appropriate to the costume. Communication of weapon size and weight is important for items pulled from pockets, concealed in bodices, or hid-den up a sleeve. Holsters must fit specific guns and are usually a prop, but must be coordinated with the belt from costumes. Undercover holsters and the appropriate gun should be provided early on to allow the costume to be fit wearing the weapon. In the case of military or police officers, the belts holding all the officer equipment requires the close collabora-tion of shops to provide the correct tactical belt for the uniform with all the accompanying and appropriate handcuffs, holsters, flashlights, keys, radios, ammunition pouch, etc. The prop shop usually provides the various items, whereas the costume shop may provide the belt itself.

When an actor is required to perform a magic trick requiring items to be concealed in the costume, the prop shop provides the magic items but must coordinate the trick requirements with the costume to insure the effects will succeed. Having both the costume and the magic tricks early in the rehearsal process allows the actor to have more time to make the effect appear smooth and natural.

Props also relies on the costume shop to provide those items for stage dressing such as clothes to pack in a suitcase or hang on a clothesline, hats and coats to dress out a coat rack in an entry hall onstage, or jewelry items handled but never worn. The "look" of those items is coordinated with both the set and the costume designers.

ELECTRICS AND SOUND

In the world of props, many items are dressed onstage to give the appearance of real items but do not need to work. However, some items need to duplicate a level of functionality. These props are called *practicals*. Practicals are any device giving the appearance of functioning as they would in real life—lighting up, emitting sound, smoking, vibrating, turning a turn table, etc. These practical props do work to some degree but are only the illusion of reality. Many are controlled from offstage to work on cue with the sound emitting from the speakers inside on cue from the soundboard operator and the light bulb illuminating when activated as part of a lighting cue from the light board. It might look like the actor is turning on the lights as he enters the room flipping on the wall switch and the sconces on the wall and the chandelier hanging in the room light up, but it's controlled offstage and not by the actor.

The *electrics department* collaborates with the prop shop for all props needing electricity to operate including table lamps, chandlers, sconces, lanterns, appliances, radios, clocks, "live" outlets, street lights, smoke effects, electrically controlled special effects—anything requiring an electrical hookup, so it can be "run" or turned on/off. Special effects such as radio-controlled and wireless DMX (digital media effects)-controlled props usually are a cross-departmental collaboration allowing both areas to explore the technology to achieve remote effects and share the expense.

Electrics will need to understand where the props requiring electricity will be located on the set to coordinate the installation of electrical power with the scenery department at load-in. Working with stage management, the prop shop can provide a close approximation of where items will be placed on a ground plan of the stage setting. Electrics personnel also need to know what voltage is required and how the prop is to be controlled. Some props may be controlled onstage by the actor, whereas others need to be controlled from the booth allowing the actor to appear to turn on a lamp, but allowing the lamp, to also be faded out with the stage lights at the end of the scene going into blackout. Other props may require control from backstage by the run crew taken from a *visual* of the actors on stage. A visual is a cue coordinated with a specific action viewed onstage and often dependent on a piece of action that is inconsistent, each performance requiring timing to be taken from what is happening onstage at that particular moment. Determination of where a cue is controlled from may not be determined until technical rehearsals, but props and electrics must work to provide the best options available.

Props with electrical hookups may require special wiring or a special plug installed to allow it to be used and controlled with the light board. Departments and theatres have varying policies about who does what and these projects should be negotiated based on who has the time and who has the skill. If the theatre is a Union house, it may be covered in the Union contract. Although the prop shop provides the actual unit such as a chandelier, wall sconce, or radio needing to light up, if the unit needs to be wired, the responsibility may fall into either shop's jurisdiction. In most cases, once the prop is built in the prop shop, the electrics department takes the prop for final wiring and, in the case of flown props such as the chandelier, coordination with the scenic department for rigging of both the unit and the cable for electricity.

Props installed on the set as part of dressing such as wall sconces, fireplace logs with a "flame," a wall clock, or shelf radio are coordinated for electrical run to be completed during set dress. The prop shop will often drill the hole for the props electrical wire to pass through to the back of the set where it is connected to the appropriate electrical run provided by the electrics department. Props set onstage near a wall in the scenery such as a floor lamp or a television can use a standard wall socket installed in the set wall. Props placed on a thrust or out away from the walls where a wall socket is unavailable might require a floor plug built into the stage floor at scenery load in. Procurement and installation of the necessary plugs and sockets and getting the electricity run to make them active is coordinated between props, electrics, and scenery.

The electrics department is often asked to wire special effects coordinated with the prop shop. Just as with chandeliers or traditional set dress items, the prop shop provides the item and electrics provides the power with the installation coordinated with the scenery load-in. This is especially important when working with anything that might give off smoke, flame, or heat, as all items near the special effect unit

A Christmas Carol

Dallas Theatre Center
Rich Gilles, Props Master

Practical List

Location	Practical	Quantity	Power	Source	
Back wall	Oil lamps	14	AC	light bulb	
	Single candles	3	AC		flicker candle
	Triple candle	3	AC		flicker candle
Street	Brazier	1	AC	light bulb	
	Lanterns on poles	2	battery		flicker candle
Office	Oil lamps	2	AC	light bulb	
	Cratchit candle	1	battery		flicker candle
	Scrooge lamp	1	battery	light bulb	
Bedroom	Oil lamp	1	AC	light bulb	
	Scrooge hand held candle	1	battery		flicker candle
	Past's hand	1	battery	LED	
Fezziwig	Chandeliers	54 to 66	AC		flicker candle
	Table candelabras	0	battery		flicker candle
Cratchit Table	Candle in chimney	1	battery		flicker candle
	Totals:	85 to 97		20	65 to 77

Flicker Candles: Have 53 good quality, 7 that are poor

FIGURE 4 List of prop practicals for *A Christmas Carol*, Dallas Theatre Center, used for coordination of use with stage management and the electrics department. Courtesy of Rich Gilles, Properties Master.

must be flame proofed or otherwise safe guarded. Costumes should also be alerted to flameproof costumes as necessary.

Similar to electrics, the *sound department* collaborates with props to bring the props to life with audio support. Radios, record players, televisions, telephones, and doorbells—anything with a speaker—require the coordination of installation with the sound department. Although props provide the actual physical source for the sound such as a radio, the sound department is responsible for making the sound emit from the source. Other times the sound department will provide support for special effects (an explosion coming from a smoke effect) or for a prop needing to look like it is making sound (a piano played by an actor who cannot play the piano, but is simply moving his hands about on the keys). This coordination of sound and props is best worked out early in the production process.

Many sound departments will prefer to simply replace the existing speaker in the prop for a different, more powerful speaker or will conceal a separate speaker near the location where the prop is used. For example, a radio might be dressed on a desk and is required to play a song at a certain point in the play. The radio's own speaker is far too small to fill the theatre, so the sound department may conceal a separate speaker on the underside of the desk or it might need to be disguised in a stack of books either on the desk or sitting on the floor beside the desk. The props department will be asked to "dress" out the area or to build the "disguise" to blend in the speaker with the stage environment. This is coordinated with the stage designer. Location of the speaker, whether inside the prop or hidden nearby in other dressing, must be coordinated with scenery as well so that audio lines can be run either up through the stage floor or installed as the scenery is being placed.

Some sound departments utilize "wireless" speakers, which allow props to emit recorded sound when running a wire isn't possible or when the prop is picked up and moved about the stage. This is especially helpful when a unit cannot be actor operated. In actor-operated situations, a small tape recorder or similar audio device can be concealed inside many props. These units make the cue dependent on the actor flipping the switch at the correct moment. A wireless speaker gives the freedom to broadcast a variety of cues or change volume from the soundboard run by the sound operator, not the onstage actor. These systems are battery operated, requiring the same considerations for battery space as well as the speaker and audio receiver. Getting the wireless unit to the prop shop and working with the sound department from an early stage in the show build allows the prop to do everything needed to support the action required by the play. Security of the unit and battery maintenance by the run crew should be considered as the prop is built and the speaker unit installed.

Previously, live sound effects were the province of the prop department. Today, sound effects are coordinated between both props and sound departments, sometimes including the music department as well in opera and music theater houses. Offstage sound may be done as a simple live effect or utilize microphone amplification to reinforce the sound of a live effect or it may be recorded. For example, a doorbell rings offstage to signal the arrival of a guest. Traditionally, the prop department would simply pull a hand-operated doorbell from stock and the run crew would ring it on cue. This can still work in small theatres where the sound of the doorbell is easily heard. However, in many theatres, the sound department controls the doorbell as a recorded cue manipulating volume, length of ring, pitch, etc. They may ask to use a doorbell from prop stock for the initial recording, but as sound effects and sound libraries expand and the digital ability to create and manipulate sound changes rapidly, the use of a live effect is becoming obsolete.

Sound departments often underscore live effects onstage with recorded sound made with the same instruments used by the actors to more effectively fill the space. The prop shop may be approached about providing instruments for those recording sessions, and most prop shops have a large collection of musical instruments to access as needed. As new instruments are requested, the purchases can be coordinated with the sound and music departments. For those theatres doing musicals or opera performances, the musicians who play the orchestration usually provide their own instruments. In some cases, the prop shop may be asked to provide an instrument not in the usual repertoire for a sound effect from the orchestra or for a performer to use on stage. The props department also may arrange for piano tuning or other support.

Collaboration between electrics, sound, and props is necessary when the prop must emit sound and also light up such as a TV set. Plays using television often face them away from the audience as they tend to draw focus away from the actors but the action of turning on the TV usually requires both sound and some minimal light effect to occur. If the TV also has to have a picture, then the video feed is coordinated with all departments as well. Video projection has grown as a scenic choice, and larger theatres may have a separate department devoted just to this area requiring props to coordinate effects and "practicals" with that department as well.

SCENERY

The scenery department and scenic paint area also overlap often into the props area. In any given design, the division of the elements as designed by the scenic designer must be divided up between props and scenery. This is often based on the size of the elements as well as the specific skills of the artisans in the different shops. Previously, in the design process, a production meeting is held to look at preliminary designs and the division of who will do what is begun even at this early stage. It is common for items to shift as the design evolves, and the design gets either more simplified or more complex. For example, the designer needs to create a downstage scenic element to establish an actor looking out a window and at first proposes a large flown header piece with a suspended window frame. Given size, method of installation (rigged), and need to visually echo the upstage architecture, it would make sense to have the unit built by scenery. But later the designer chooses to establish the window by simply rigging a drapery swag hanging above the stage where the window would be with a window bench placed on the floor. The drape and the furniture piece are obviously props and the rigging of the hanging drape would be coordinated with scenery.

Sometimes the lines are not so easily defined. Instances where props and scenery intersect often have to do with artisan skill sets and shop workloads. For example, determining responsibilities when large carved statuary is required, trees and other landscaping are needed, or when a large part of the stage space is completed with rugs or textured "landfill" are all frequently negotiable situations. It could go either way depending on budget, artisan availability and skill, and what else the shops are being asked to complete or build.

Props and scenery need to coordinate the movement of scene changes. Talking through what has to move first and how props get safely on and off stage as well as guaranteeing the security of actors and crew is an important consideration for both shops and stage management. Storage space backstage is often tight, requiring both shops to be involved in how things track, where prop run tables can be placed, and how props can be preset or struck off during the show.

Props flying in or being rigged must be coordinated with the scene shop staff person responsible for rigging. The prop shop should be working with the technical director to build props having appropriate structure and points for either a single or a multiple point fly and to be properly weighted, neither too heavy nor cumbersome to fly or so light weight that the prop cannot offset the rigging requirements. Size and spacing are often critical factors. Ensuring the prop to be flown has proper clearance among the multitude of other things being flown or rigged must be coordinated between scenery, electrics, and prop shop. A large three-dimensional chandelier may need to become a two-armed "flat" chandelier to have it fly between scenic pieces and electrical battens. All these decisions are done in collaboration with the scenic designer and lighting designer as well.

Props should make any requests for special building considerations to accommodate set dressing in advance of scenic unit completion. For example, if the prop shop knows placement of pictures or wall sconces on set walls, the scene shop can install backings allowing for extra support in those areas if given the necessary measurements and information to install them during the build. The prop shop also should coordinate the dressing of elements being flown or inaccessible from the floor with the scenery load-in. Hopefully, the technical director is in communication with the properties director and production stage manager about any minor changes in things like sizes of windows or changes in door openings, which may impact the building of props like curtains or props carried in and out through the door. Technical rehearsal is not the time to discover the door opening was shrunk three inches making the entrance of a wheelbarrow loaded with suitcases impossible.

The production meeting allows both departments to communicate any concerns or confirm changes impacting the other department's work or product.

Props also needs to be in discussion about built-in items such as window seats, bookshelves, kitchen cabinets, or fireplaces to insure they will be able to support the dressing weight and function as needed to support the action of the play. Getting the sizes of the actual built objects and not relying on designer drawings is critical, as the scene shop must often adjust dimensions slightly for budget or ease of building purposes. If the prop shop needs to have bookshelves to support the weight of real books, the scene shop should be warned early in the process so that appropriate bracing of the wall unit is planned and strong shelves can be built. Visits to each other's shops are also a great way to confirm vital information. For example, the prop shop should go to the scene shop and measure the window seat unit before it builds the pillow sitting on the seat to double check the size is correct or the scene shop could ask to see the wall sconces needing to be installed so appropriate bracing can be planned as the wall units are built.

Coordination of the installation of "practical" elements is critical. This is especially true when re-creating something like a kitchen on stage and the running of water, electrical, and gas lines for a stove, sink, refrigerator, etc. must be coordinated between multiple areas of production.

The *scenic art* department is responsible for the painting and finishing of scenic items. Some prop departments have their own painters, but collaboration will still be necessary to visually coordinate the scenery with the props, and the scenic artists often share paint and processes with the prop shop artisans. The tone, texture, and finish of furniture should be compatible with the scenic items. Some shows require the elements to match, and in those cases, the scenic artist will often paint both scenery and props. In situations where the scenic artist is also responsible for painting a prop, it is extremely important to discuss the surface preparation of the prop, how the prop will ultimately be used (use relates to wear and tear on the painted finish), dry time required impacting readiness of the prop for rehearsal, and potential touch up and maintenance concerns. Scenic artists often are the "craftsmen," filling the artistic space between the props and scenery shops when those large carving projects or landscape projects are required. Scenic artists also often come to the prop shop for collaboration on stencil production or pattern making requiring the finer tools or the computer graphic support found in the prop shop.

Working on a show with the other specialty artists found in the various shops around the theatre is where the collaborative nature of theatre-making sets the theatre world apart from other trades utilizing similar skill sets. As the artists share in the process of solving the problems by offering solutions, using their ideas and skills, and working together to build the world of the play, the enormous creative support provided behind the scenes adds a dimension to the production unimaginable to the average theatre viewer.

Chapter 7

The Build Process

Once the prop list is updated and all the information from various sources compiled, the "build" can begin in earnest. Depending on the availability and interest of the designer, the properties director juggles the decision of how to complete each prop depending on what is in stock, the availability of items in the community from other organizations or theatres, what is within the skill of the prop shop personnel to build, the advisability of altering stock pieces, the availability and expense of materials to build the props, the necessity of having the item in rehearsal quickly, and/or the expense of purchasing the item or materials needed to build the item. Every variable of that decision-making process can change as the prop build progresses.

In the best-case scenario, design information is communicated far in advance of the build, allowing the budgeting and preliminary work to be completed weeks before the show actually enters the shop. Some theatres work six to eight months in advance of shows starting to be built. This is often the case for opera and musical theatre where designers are contracted and designs completed in a more timely manner than the regional theatre process. In a regional theatre, the designs for a show often dribble in with preliminary information available a month or two out from start of build and final drawings arriving just in time for the build to begin. If designers could only get the design process completed earlier, the results would be so much better!

The design deadlines and important production dates are often communicated in a *production calendar* or *production timeline*. The time-line calls out each date for design meetings/deadlines, drawing due dates, shop specific deadlines (furniture pull, fabric shopped, paint samples complete, etc.), first rehearsal, designer residencies, load-in, technical rehearsals, and all other relevant production information up to opening night. The production timeline allows each shop to have expectations for information, holding the designer to the specified date. If the deadline is missed, the production manager can step in to push the project along, explaining the budgetary and calendar consequences.

Back in the days before the instant access of computers, information about props often came later in the build than other areas, far after the decisions about what the set looks like and the drawings were completed. Having the information at the same time as other areas, a preliminary budget can be created showing what has to be built, and the anticipated expense of the build allows a negotiation to occur on what items should have priority and alternate solutions offered. Having drawings allows the shop to plan the build taking into consideration the difficulty of what is proposed to be built balanced against the other items on the prop list to be pulled, rented, or bought. Keeping an open communication with the designer during the process and being proactive to advance the process, whether through finding pictorial research showing various options, pulling things for consideration from stock that could be modified, doing sketches/drawings for response from the designer, "swatching" upholstery/curtain fabrics for consideration and getting character fabric swatches from costumes to coordinate the look of things—whatever needs to be done to get decisions made, the properties director should do.

Regardless of the venue or the company, large prop items such as furniture are defined at an early stage when the "bigger picture" of scenery and the overall design are being determined. These large set items and the requested set dressing tends to be the focus at the beginning of most builds until rehearsal notes start giving more specifics about the hand props. Fortunately, hand props are usually the easier things to find or make and can be worked on around the larger prop items in production once the requests are made. Each artisan will have a balance of large and small projects to work on in any given build allowing them opportunities to create props most specific to their talent and interest from the large to the very smallest items.

The prop director has only four real options to juggle in completing the prop list regardless of set props, dressing, or a hand prop. Each prop may be completed in one or a combination of the following:

PULL   BORROW   BUILD   BUY

PULLING FROM STOCK

First, looking to see what is in the prop stock and can be pulled offers a fast and usually inexpensive solution to finding the prop. Many theatres maintain a large inventory of items used repeatedly in the productions, and a slight modification can be made specific to each show. Having a prop stock saves thousands of dollars in hand prop procurement alone and can still offer a variety of choices. Many items such as kitchen pots or pans, china, glassware, period magazines, ashtrays, garden ware, and decorative objects can be used repeatedly on stage for a variety

FIGURE 1 Glassware/kitchen hand prop storage for Actors Theatre of Louisville prop shop. Courtesy of Mark Walston, Properties Director.

of productions even without alteration. Paper props like newspapers, magazines, or letters built for one show, when saved in stock, are a quick pull when dressing is needed for the next show. Stock picture frames can have new photos added. Greenery and floral arrangements can be rearranged and reused. Blankets, bed sheets, pillows, or other linens need only a quick washing and they're ready for the stage.

Selecting stock furniture and reupholstering it or making slight modifications to the "look" allow the designer to make the choice specific to the show and save having to build or buy the items. Owning certain classic silhouettes of furniture means it will be used repeatedly by simply changing the fabric or frame color or combining the items in different configurations to create a new look. Even if all the pieces cannot be pulled, often the savings offered by using *some* stock furniture allows for a specialty piece to be invested in to complement existing stock pieces and add to stock for future productions.

Having a computerized *inventory* of furniture stock has become increasingly handy. Many designers are not on-site and being able to post photos and dimensions on a website for the designer to view stock pieces under consideration allows for quick communication of available pieces. Using software to create an inventory with pictures of each piece of furniture along with information such as dimensions, upholstery,

FIGURE 2 Actors Theatre of Louisville furniture storage with computerized prop inventory hangtags. Courtesy of Mark Walston, Properties Director.

finish, physical condition, previous show use, time period, etc. allows for items to be easily "searched" in the database by the entry of any particular characteristic such as "bench" and "wooden" to find all the various wooden benches in stock. Some theatre companies keep their entire inventories online, whereas others prefer to select options and create a "cloud" dropbox online for the designer to see the selected group.

Keeping the inventory updated and accurate is critical. As pieces are bought or stock items changed, updated photographs and information should be added to the computerized inventory. This is often assigned as part of one of the artisan's job responsibilities during strike.

Having a similar inventory of hand props would be helpful but impractical. There are literally thousands of hand props in most company's storage and maintaining that filing would be a full-time job alone. Managing the hand prop stock and keeping it organized is an intensive and time-consuming project without even attempting to track all the changes, adds, and breakage coming with producing a season. Simply going to prop storage and selecting what will work best or collecting several options for the designer to choose from is a quick and easy solution to start the process. It's kind of fun to just walk the aisles and "shop" for what is in stock. Sometimes the most amazing possibilities present themselves.

FIGURE 3 Prop storage at Actors Theatre of Louisville. Courtesy of Mark Walston, Properties Director.

When pulling, it is important to keep an open mind about what discoveries might occur as props are sorted and pulled. Oftentimes, it is possible to discover something that might be easily modified or utilized as a *part* of a built piece. Fabric sewn as curtains for a previous show can be modified into a bedspread or dyed a different color to work in the present show. A wooden box can be covered in fabric and with leather straps added would transform into a period trunk. Almost anything can become a lamp. A letter handwritten for one show can become a "proclamation" with the addition of a gold seal and some ribbon. Look with fresh eyes and think about the possibilities of what can be done, how it can be altered, the "what if …" of pulling an item and using it in a different way.

Pulling dressing is an adventure into character analysis. Think who is this person? What are their hobbies? What kind of books would they read? Do they garden or enjoy cooking? Where have they traveled? How old are they? What is their religious affiliation? What is their favorite sports team/artist/recording artist? Answering these questions can help define what items to pull for shelf decoration, to hang on the walls, to fill the niches and spaces around the set needing prop fill. When pulling dressing, it's a common practice to pull a wide variety of items for final selection on set dress day. Remember to include different shapes, colors, textures, and patterns unless the design is a specific palette or "look." Variety creates interest.

Once the pull is completed, items are moved to the prop shop for alteration or finishing. This may include additional reinforcing to support the specific action of the production, a change in upholstery to fit into the color scheme, or a simple clean and polish to restore the original luster of the finish. In more drastic cases, a stock piece may be significantly altered to create a different silhouette, to lower the back or extend the length of a piece of furniture, or may be disassembled to use parts to create an entirely new piece. This choice usually lies with the properties director working in collaboration with the artisans and the designer to prioritize what can be done on the budget allowed within the limitations of talent and time.

Any alteration or modification of stock items invariably requires some materials to be found or purchased whether it's wood, upholstery supplies, paint, trim, or craft supplies. The artisan/s involved in completing the project must determine what is needed and communicate the quantity to the properties director. Working with the shopper/buyer to determine pricing and availability within the budget limits, the material list is prioritized and becomes part of the buy list.

BORROW

Those theatres fortunate enough to have other organizations within a short driving distance often have a relationship allowing the sharing of stock items between their companies. Storage space is always critical, and although having a stock available is very handy, the necessity of maintaining stock is always limited by the availability and accessibility of the space it is stored in. Establishing and maintaining a mutually beneficial loan agreement allows theatres to use what is available at other companies and need not buy/store the same items.

Some non-theatre organizations such as furniture or antique stores are willing to lend out items from their floor stock for credit in the program or for a small rental fee. Borrowing an item from an individual is also a possibility; finding the person who has a personal collection of whatever specific item is needed is like finding a gold mine. In all cases, those relationships must be guarded with great care and stewardship. It only takes one instance of a damaged or lost item to sever a relationship with an individual or organization, so extraordinary care and consideration must be given to anything borrowed.

Having insurance coverage for *any* item that is borrowed is *mandatory*. Many organizations have some kind of insurance policy covering items lost, stolen, or broken, but many items being borrowed fall under the deductible and, in the case where something gets damaged, lost, or stolen, then the full expense must be covered. Hopefully, the loss would be covered under a contingency budget, but it might come out of the props budget and can be a costly unanticipated expense. All too often theatres seem willing to take the risk for those items falling under their insurance deductible believing it is cheaper. Because many deductibles are in the $500 or even $1000 range, many borrowed props would not have a viable claim against the insurance policy anyway because they cost less than that to replace or repair.

Determining whether an item should be borrowed must always be measured against the potential for it to be damaged. Using a borrowed item onstage requires notification of its value to stage management and anyone who handles the item so that all appropriate precaution can be exercised. It is especially important to inform the production manager in cases where borrowed items are under a greater risk of being damaged. This allows anticipation of what could be an additional expense and acceptance of the potential for budget overrun. This mentality often justifies the expense of *not* borrowing an item, but finding a different solution especially when the risk is high that the item might be damaged. Many organizations are reluctant to loan out props if they know that they will be shifted or used in a way that might endanger them. If there is a potential for damage, it's probably better *not* to borrow an item rather than risk losing a borrowing source because an item was damaged in the show.

For items at a low risk, which seem appropriate for borrowing, a standard *borrowing form* is often used to help document ownership and value as well as the expectations of how the object will be used, stored, cared for, and returned safely during the length of its use.

This is especially important for those items qualifying for coverage under the theatres insurance policy, as most insurers require some kind of documentation for reimbursement. Please check with your risk management person for details on your theatre's insurance coverage and appropriate policy requirements. Check *before* bringing a borrowed item into the building and certainly before putting it on stage or into rehearsal.

Any borrowed items should be cared for as if they were the theatre's own property or better. If you are going to borrow furniture, be sure to arrive on time and in an appropriate vehicle complete with moving dollies and moving pads to protect items while in transit. While borrowing

Theatre Prop Borrowing Form

LOANED TO:_____CONTACT:_____

ADDRESS:_____

PHONE:_(_____)_____   DATE PICKED UP:___/___/____

PRODUCTION:_____   TO BE RETURNED:___/___/___

The Theatre Properties Department is loaning the following items for use in your production/ workshop/class as listed above. You personally, and for your organization (when applicable), by accepting these items and signing this loan form, agree to the following conditions:

1. Appointments must be made with the Props Master to look thru props storage, for PICK-UP and RETURN of props. If an appointment is missed by more than 15 minutes, it must be rescheduled at the discretion of the prop shop.
2. All items will be kept in a safe and secure location at all times.
3. All items will be returned in the same condition as they left prop storage, excluding **normal** wear and tear.
4. If modifications are desired, permission must be obtained from the Properties Manager in advance. Any "modifications" made without prior permission will be viewed as damage to the specific item, and repair charges will be accessed.
5. All repairs to damaged items must be completed by the Theatre prop shop (based on an hourly fee plus materials) unless other arrangements are made with the Properties Manager in advance of any actual repairs being started. REPEAT: Repairs done without permission will be considered "damage".
6. The borrowing organization is responsible for the stated value of any item that is lost, stolen, or damaged beyond reasonable repairs. Damaged items remain the property of Theatre even when total replacement cost is accessed.
7. The Theatre Properties Manager must be notified A.S.A.P. after any item is damaged. Please do not wait until the end of your rental to let us know.
8. All items are to be returned on or before the date specified on this form. Props must be checked in by the Properties Manager at the time of their return. REPEAT: If an appointment is missed by more than 15 minutes, it must be rescheduled at the discretion of the prop shop.
9. Renter is responsible for all shipping fees, moving and pick up arrangements. Items must be insured for stated value if returned by shipment

CONTACT _____

Returned: Donation due: ☐

Notes: paid: ☐

Item	Description	Value	Fee

| Checks should be made out to: THEATRE COMPANY | | TOTAL DUE: | |

FIGURE 4 Standard borrowing form.

glass items or fragile pieces, come prepared with appropriate boxes and packing materials.

All items should be safely stored, maintained, and cared for with the highest regard. Stage management and the run crew should be given all appropriate information on how to handle the borrowed prop and informed of any special considerations for its safekeeping or use. At strike, if any alterations were done (with the owner's permission), they should be restored to the original basis before returning unless explicit permission was granted to keep it in the altered condition. Any fabric items should be dry cleaned or washed. Furniture should be wiped down, vacuumed, or cleaned as needed. Hand props should be properly cleaned and wrapped in storage boxes for transportation and delivery. It is always wise to call ahead and arrange for prop return guaranteeing the props can be handed off with a minimum of inconvenience for all involved.

In the worst case, despite all precautions and planning, when something has been stolen, broken, or damaged, notify the production manager or risk management office so that the insurance coverage process can begin. This may mean repair to the item or complete replacement. When replacement is impossible, then full reimbursement will need to be made to the owner for the cost of the borrowed item. Equally important is notification of the original owner who lent the items telling what happened, the extent of the damage, and what is being done to rectify the situation. *Never* wait until you are returning a borrowed item to tell the person who lent it to you that something happened to it. Nothing will ruin a relationship faster than returning damaged items. Be honest. Apologize. Tell them how the problem will be solved and how the prop is going to be repaired or replaced.

BUILD

Building props specific for the production is part of most builds. Designers may give scaled drawings detailing the specific shape, finish, and construction for the prop. Often designers communicate what they want by using a photo or set of photos demonstrating the desired look and the information about size or finish communicated by notation on the photos. Other times, designers rely on the properties director to manage the building of props based on verbal descriptions of what the prop should look like and may or may not be accompanied by a rough sketch or photocopy of research for confirmation. Each properties director develops a way of working the communication between the designer and the shop, and some are more likely to step into the designer's role of research and creation with only a confirmation of design choice coming from the scenic designer. Others strongly feel that it is the designer's role to do that work and rely on the designer for all information ... hopefully before the show goes into technical rehearsals. All too often props is left to the last, and getting information from the designer is difficult, forcing the properties director to take a more active role in determining what things look like.

Information about props is expected to be submitted as part of the preliminary design ideas and certainly should be included in the final design package. Having preliminary prop information allows budgeting to occur in a timely manner in conjunction with scenery, and the entire package can be modified or approved by seeing the whole project. In addition to the scenery information, the final design package should include a furniture plot, set prop requirements and major dressing, any prop drawings for built items, and all necessary research.

Most hand prop information is not included at this time but evolves during the rehearsal process. As designers become increasingly busy, production managers have begun to establish firm deadlines to establish timely design information submissions. Both the directors and the designers are made aware of the deadlines. This should facilitate the communication and creative process to move along so that the information on the build can be moved to the shop on schedule.

The properties director assigns projects to be built by the various artisans in the shop, and it is their responsibility to ask questions and carry the responsibility for completion of the prop to the satisfaction of the

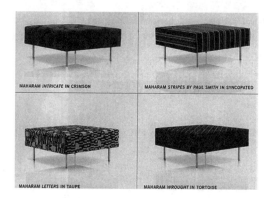

FIGURE 5   Preliminary information/research from a catalog to show basic structure and upholstery choice.

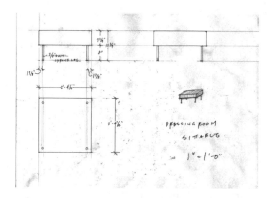

FIGURE 6   Prop drawing giving dimensions and general notes.

FIGURE 7   Full-stage shot showing furniture dressed in the scene.
Figures 5–7 courtesy of Lisa Schlenker, Properties Director, Skylight Opera Theatre. Photos in Figure 6 and 7 by Takeshi Kata, Scenic Designer for *La Traviata*.

designer. The properties director and the artisan discuss what processes to build with and what materials should be used. The priority of completion is set within the overall build of all items and may be moved about depending on the changes coming from rehearsal. Some items may be built to a certain level of completion and sent into rehearsal to be used for a time before being returned to complete the final paint finish or upholstery making it ready for load-in and technical rehearsals. This allows valuable response for specialty built items while time is still available to make alterations as well as helping the actors understand how the final prop might differ from a rehearsal prop they had been using.

Every show requires props to be altered or built depending on stock availability and the requirements of the script. Creating objects with a specific size or weight is a common request. Finding real objects may satisfy the visual look, but if the item is too heavy to be easily shifted or the stage space requires a low back or a different length, then a build or modification may be necessary. Many built furniture pieces have additional bracing or even a metal reinforcing structure added to allow for the extra abuse prop furniture encounters.

Built hand props such as newspapers with specific headlines or family photographs using the actor's faces can require extra setup time. Using the computer has freed the manipulation of graphics from the old "cut and glue down" to a click of the mouse, making downloads of period documents, labels, and even whole newspapers possible. Adding in a photo of an actor or typing in a specific headline is possible using any of the various graphics programs and printing the paper out on a plotter or quality printer. Adobe Photoshop and Adobe Illustrator are two common programs used, and many shops now have an area with a scanner, wide format printer, and computer to generate these kinds of props.

Some items such as handwritten letters can also be produced on a computer, but the conformity of the machine makes them appear computer generated even when a "handwriting" script is used. If the letter might be seen by the audience, having calligraphy skills and knowing how to write in a period style allows the prop to have the appropriate look and feel with dark ink splotches and all. In the case where *many* letters are required, after the original is completed and approved, more can be made using a photocopier to duplicate the document. Paper size can be modified after copying to make documents fit period, appropriate paper sizes, or colors. A wide variety of papers in various weights and colors as well as textures are available for use in photocopiers allowing quick paper prop creations.

Building a prop also means making it look like it belongs in the world of the play. Understanding how to distress wood, fabric, metal, and other materials is necessary to instill props with a history. Once props are built, the final step is usually making it fit into the world of the other props by giving it the correct patina, polish, paint finish, or even wiping down with dirt or mud. Fabric might be bleached or toned with dyes, tattered or worn down with a rasp or sureform, and trim pulled free and stretched. Upholstery is often layered to create a saggy cushion or flattened for a look of great age and use. Design Master Floral Sprays, which stick to almost all materials, are often used to tone and distress prop items. Glossy wood tone is a personal favorite as it gives the perfect "dirt" tone to most materials. Krylon clear flat sealer is an alternative treatment to take the edge of newness off of many surfaces.

Building a prop can be a time-consuming, expensive, and laborious process, and accurately managing the fabricated items within the context of the whole build often determines the choice made between building or borrowing an item if it can be found in the community. On the other hand, building props enriches the prop stock as items are added to both furniture and hand props expanding on what will be available for productions in the future. More importantly, building is often the only way you can create a specific prop fitting exactly what the designer envisioned and the show requires.

BUY

Shopping is a necessary part of *every* build. Within every good prop person is a shopper just waiting to discover an incredible bargain! Best of all, it's using someone else's money! Sometimes it might be the procurement of materials to modify stock items or to build a prop. It might be buying specific items particular to the production and requiring no or very little modification. Some things are a quick trip to the nearest lumberyard, whereas other items require the shopper/buyer to spend days tracking down a requested item with a particular look or having a specific function.

Utilization of the Internet for specialty shopping sites online has dramatically changed the way the prop shop functions and increases the ease of finding things. The Internet makes shopping convenient and opens the entire world as the market for procuring items. With easy search links, the ability to find even the most absurd request becomes increasingly possible.

Shopping on the Internet requires a few simple security rules to safeguard the credit card and other personal information. Online web sites may be the portal for a large company also having retail sites, but it is more commonly a shop with no local footprint. You can't drive there and see the product but must trust the description and photos available online. Many stores offer more selection online than what they carry locally, so checking online can open more choices. Shopping online saves the drive time as well as the expense of driving to the store. Shopping online at trusted sites with return policies and a proven shipping department makes the process simple and safe. Always check to confirm the companies' return policy. Some companies allow returns to a store even when the items were bought online saving return shipping and handling fees. Newer online companies, while unknown and perhaps lacking a retail store, can be equally safe, but it's best to review their buying policies and be sure a full refund is possible if the merchandise is unacceptable. Many sites have contact information with a phone number allowing you to call and talk to someone or offer a "live chat" feature on their website, so information can be confirmed before purchase.

When placing an order, be sure to review all the information checking for amount, color, size, shipping information, billing information, etc. Most sites will confirm the entire order before asking for a final buy button to be pushed completing the sale. Print off or save to a folder the receipt and any information about anticipated delivery dates or seller contact information. Most online sites operate using order codes allowing an update on shipping or where the order is in process by going to the website and typing in the code. Once the item has been shipped, many companies will send an e-mail giving a tracking number to follow the shipment. This is especially helpful if working against a deadline and the package doesn't arrive in a timely fashion. Many sites require the buyer to register and set a password while also requesting delivery and credit card information. Be sure to write down your registration name and password in a secure place so that accessing the site in the future is easy.

Before entering credit card information, confirm whether the site is a registered secure site. Oftentimes, these sites have a lock image in the corner as well as language confirming the site has appropriate protocols to keep credit card information safe from hackers or others who may want to access delivery or billing information. Although most credit card companies offer fraud alerts and protective coverage in case credit card information gets stolen, it is the responsibility of the credit card holder to monitor activity on the card by scanning statements for unauthorized purchases and alerting the company when something is wrong. Policies vary for cardholder liability, so check out the fine print in those agreements to know your card exposure.

Before the Internet, having a large resource file was critical. The properties director or, in larger shops, the shopper artisan was known for the depth of the card file filled with resources, knowing where to find any item or having a person in the community known to the shopper/buyer who can connect to the needed item. Maintaining a long list of resources both locally and via the Internet is critical. It's always helpful to "know somebody who knows somebody" when trying to solve a particular prop problem. And as is often the case in theatre, shows are repeated. Someone has done the show before or solved this particular problem. Knowing whom to call can cut down on a lot of time-consuming research and development. For prop directors, the most direct route is to put the question out on a prop building/production/theatre web site. If they are a member of *Society of Properties Artisans/Managers* (SPAM), it is easy to email the question to the group, and within hours, someone in the group (and often several, if not many) will reply with a solution. For more information on SPAM, please go to the webpage: http://propmasters.org.

A prop shopper quickly becomes familiar with the local resources available in the immediate shopping area. The telephone's Yellow Pages offer quick access to many businesses and individuals offering services or materials used in the prop shop. Good telephone communication skills are critical for determining what is available locally. As purchasing relationships develop and the shopper's knowledge of where to buy and what is available grows, the ease of shopping for many supplies becomes easier. Knowing where to find things in the community is critical for successful shopping, and strong "people skills" are necessary to maintain relationships with the shops and companies the theatre frequents for supplies. Getting discounts or special pricing as a nonprofit organization can save hundreds of dollars over the season build, and repeat customers are more likely to get these accommodations. Businesses are also often willing to "hold" an item while a designer is consulted based on previous positive business experiences.

The shopper must develop the "designer's" eye, making decisions in the field for appropriate choices on props. Working from the designer's drawings, collages, or verbal descriptions, the shopper locates the various items needed for the show as well as the materials needed for the shop. The shopper is also the one taking and picking up tools needing repair or running over to the off-site storage area to search for props needing to be pulled.

The modern prop shopper has many more technological tools available as well. With most cell phones having a built-in camera, it's easy to snap a photo and email it off for confirmation to the designer or the properties director. This is especially helpful when fabric shopping as a photo can show design repeat, scale, and even texture. When furniture shopping, it's easy to photograph many choices for consideration and take an accompanying photo of the price tag, fabric content, and dimension sheet keeping all the information organized. If the designer is "online," the communication can be immediate, otherwise it does entail a return to the store for purchasing following affirmation to buy, but that is usually better than purchasing and then needing to return an item.

Given the responsibility of purchasing, it's important for the shopper to be organized with receipts and petty cash. The shopper is accountable for the purchases made and for tracking the receipts to be entered in the budget in communication with the properties director.

The prop list has been reviewed, and every prop is notated with at least one way to solve the problem. The shopping list is made (at least for now). Stock has been reviewed and items pulled. Artisans are figuring out how to proceed with the individual projects assigned to them. Items to be borrowed are confirmed and pick-up times established. The build is on.

Most LORT theatres tend to have a four to six week rehearsal period. This corresponds to the shop "build" as well. As the run crew goes into technical rehearsals on a show, the prop shop artisans move to start the build on the next production. The properties director juggles back and forth between the two shows—one getting ready to open and one going into rehearsal—supervising the shop as well as attending technical rehearsals. According to a SPAM survey, the property director may work over 60 hours a week during the technical rehearsal week shift attending nightly technical rehearsals and running the shop during the day. Hopefully, the shop has been given enough information completing the preliminary work on the next show to allow the shop artisans to move forward. Regional theatres also tend to have multiple performance spaces with the prop shop juggling several "builds" at a time, so it might also be the case that an artisan or two get moved over to start on a different show even before the one show is loaded in for technical rehearsals. Companies producing in several venues might utilize a large artisan staff supervised by prop masters for each particular show who report to the properties director to have multiple builds happening at one time in the shop. On the other hand, small companies with only one person in the shop or perhaps with a single artisan rarely get the luxury of getting a jump start on a show and are into significant overtime when opening multiple shows.

Using the divisions of build, buy, borrow, and pull, a prop show build can be accomplished bringing an on-time, on-budget, to-the-satisfaction-of-the-designer conclusion. Working as part of the team in the shop whether as artisan, shopper, or properties director, the ultimate goal is to manage the work load, so all involved are equally engaged, to build high-quality professional level props fulfilling the action needed while creating the designed "look" and to be ready to move into the theatre for the technical rehearsals when all parts of the production come together. The show moves out of the shop and on to the stage, into the hands of the run crew. The juggle of the build and final closure on the show build is ended at opening … then, on to the next build, the next juggle of what to build, buy, borrow, and pull.

Chapter 8

The Production/Tech Process

During the weeks of the build, the prop shop is in full production mode finalizing the set props, pulling and finding dressing pieces, and building hand props. Stage management and actors are invited to drop in and see the props they will be using on stage. The designer is often "in house" and available for all the last minute tweaking and decision making. The final coordination between the other shops is completed, and the production calendar breaks down into specific task-oriented goals.

Every theatre has a "technical rehearsal to opening" sequence, but within that time frame, many of the same goals must be accomplished. These include: set load-in, set dress, prop check-in, spacing rehearsal, technical rehearsal, dress rehearsal, opening, run, and strike. It is a logical process layering each level of production on the show, working toward opening night, anticipating the run, and the eventual strike of the show.

Load-in and *Tech* week are the time when all the elements must come together and, hence, can be fraught with differing goals from the various production areas. Time on stage becomes precious. Electrics need time to hang and focus. The scenic artist needs to do touch-up work on the scenery or paint the floor. The prop shop wants time to set the furniture with stage management and dress out the set. The actors want to move from the rehearsal hall onto the stage to become accustomed to the space. Preplanning and establishing priorities allows this schedule to build logically and give time for everyone. This is often worked out in the weekly production meeting far in advance of the actual load-in weeks and is monitored and managed by the production manager. When the schedule needs to be changed, the production manager must juggle the priorities to insure the needs are met and each department still retains at least some time on stage to perform their work. Being an advocate for the prop department and understanding some times that things just can't be planned for and things go awry, the properties director must be able to plan for an efficient and prioritized set dress to protect the time needed on stage.

LOAD-IN

All set dressing, hand props, and furniture will need to be onstage for the first technical rehearsal. Set dress can start as soon as scenery and the paint department have the architecture of the set in place and when further construction or painting won't jeopardize the dressing.

In some theatres, set dress is requested to be complete before *lighting focus* because stage dressing may impact specials. As the crew focuses the lights, props such as foliage dressed outside a door, drapery over a window, or a hanging chandelier can limit the area trying to be lit. Having the dressing completed before the focus happens prevents a need for re-focus. At the very least, inform the master electrician of anticipated dressing conflicts. More importantly, it is helpful for all props, including furniture, to be onstage for *light level set*. The colors, textures, and shadows created by the props can dramatically change the appearance of the stage space once the stage lights are illuminated.

Prop check-in with stage management and prop run crew should be scheduled before first tech to go over all the props, to show how they work, and to discuss any special needs or instructions on use, storage, or cleaning. Some organizations have a *shift rehearsal* allowing the run crew personnel to practice presets, set and prop cues for onstage internal/act changes, and fly cues before actors come onstage. Practicing these types of shifts works best when *all* the crew is available, and in some cases, actors assist in scene changes by either carrying off props or bringing on props. In those cases, the shifts must be rehearsed during the technical rehearsal time when everyone is available or by finding someone to stand in for the actor during the shift rehearsal.

In the best of all circumstances, most of the props will have already been in rehearsal or a close facsimile used, allowing stage management and the actors to have an easy transition to the stage.

Furniture props are set on stage in collaboration with stage management. Minor adjustments during the rehearsal process often invalidate the designer's original floor plan of where the furniture was to be set and taking measurements in the rehearsal hall to transfer the same relationships to the stage is helpful. Following preliminary placement, it is common for the director and the designer to alter where things were set to allow for sight lines or better flow around the space before the first technical rehearsal.

Stage managers often tape markings on the floor to create a way to track where the furniture is placed utilizing different colors for different scenes. This process is called *spiking*. Once the furniture placement is finalized and prior to opening, the tape is trimmed to smaller tabs or even painted so that it becomes invisible to the audience yet still present enough for the shift crew to follow. Furniture is spiked even in shows where the furniture is not shifted allowing the floor to be swept, mopped, and furniture replaced accurately. Spiking the furniture guarantees the placement for crucial lighting cues as well as guaranteeing the spacing between all furniture pieces, stage edge, steps, walls, entrances, or exits remains the same for the stage action.

FIGURE 1   Stage Manager Brandon Campbell checks measurements from rehearsal for placement of furniture with the prop shop during set dress. University of Wisconsin–Milwaukee.

Set dressing is often coordinated with the scenic designer present for the final placement/dressing decisions. Although some things can be completed at the same time as a light level set or while scenery is working on backing flats or securing trim, adequate time should be allowed for the dressing of the stage and having safe lighting and working conditions are important.

Scheduling a "set dress" time, especially on a realistic set with time-consuming picture placement, curtain hanging and draping, bookcases to be filled, rugs stapled down, and furniture placed and dressed out, is just as important a part of the load-in as hanging the lighting instruments or putting in the scenery. Adequate time must be scheduled. To use the time most efficiently, the prop shop staff can utilize several strategies to be prepared to make the set dress easier. Items can be "predressed" in the shop, establishing a final look and photographed for reference, can be "undressed" into labeled boxes, so once the piece is on stage, can be quickly dressed out from the box specific to its location. Having boxes of "like" items such as books, kitchen utensils, "chochtka" décor, photographs in frames, etc. available to be placed as needed speeds up the dressing process. Pictures should be framed, and all the necessary hardware attached for all wall décor so that hanging is facilitated. When filling out an exterior scene, having bags of mulch or moss and small artificial plants set in plaster bases for easy placing fills in gaps quickly completing the look. Many shops use a portable tool cart with an organized hardware kit including a variety of screws, hangers, nails, floral putty, felt guards, wire, and tools to solve any installation or dressing needs.

It is a smart practice to do the "hem" on curtains once the set has been installed or at the very least, once the actual window is built, and accurate measurements can be taken to guarantee that the length from rod to floor is final. Drawings from the designer are often altered slightly by the scene shop, and a difference of a few inches is disastrous when determining the finished length of drapery. Having a stock of safety pins or hem clips to pin up the curtains to their final length and out of the way for the onstage rehearsal is necessary unless adequate time is available to complete the sewing before first tech.

Prop check-in usually occurs in the prop shop with representatives from stage management and the props run crew as needed. Each prop is loaded into the rolling prop run cabinet or into carts to be moved to the stage and placed on secure run tables. For those theatre companies with the production studio located in another building or even across town, props must be boxed up, loaded into rolling "run" cabinets, or in some way safely transported to the theatre. Prop check-in is then conducted at the theatre as the props are unloaded and unpacked.

Prop check-in is where the prop list and numbering system prove especially helpful. As each number is called out, each prop is explained, and any concerns about maintenance or handling are addressed. If, for example, the prop is a diary which the actor reads and writes in nightly, the prop crew may utilize different colored bookmarks to assist the actor in finding the specific written passages or may have cut corners off from the page to make those specific pages easier to find. The pages getting written on each night may be only temporarily affixed and require additional pages to be added each night. Showing this to the run crew and explaining the use guarantees consistency and understanding of how the prop is to be used as well as what nightly maintenance is required to keep the diary consistent for each performance. It might also be something as simple as how to store an item, so it is more easily maintained such as rolling a flag or banner so that it doesn't get wrinkled or have fold lines. Furniture pieces may have known weaknesses, and the crew should be alerted to check those pieces carefully to detect breakage or damage. This is especially important in a show where the furniture is abused or used in a way causing extraordinary strain on the furniture joints, legs, or arms.

As the props are checked in, it is common to sort them by preset or storage location with accompanying paperwork for documenting tracking. This is easily done using the item name or number. Hand props are checked into the run crew for placement in secure cabinets until it is time to set them out on the run tables for the technical rehearsal. A *run table* is the location where hand props are set before the start of the show for actors to pick up or drop off items used in their particular scenes. These are usually set up and maintained by stage management or the props run crew.

Once all the props are checked in and the set dressed, the prop shop is ready for technical rehearsals and for the actors to inhabit the space.

TECHNICAL REHEARSAL

Technical rehearsals are the times scheduled for when all the elements of production are layered onto the rehearsed performance. Actors are in the stage space defined by the designer, using the props, and eventually wearing costumes and enveloped in the lighting and sound effects. Technical rehearsals are when everything has to come together and, while often a time of some anxiety and stress, are also immensely rewarding when the elements start to really work and the play comes to life.

The first rehearsal where the real props are used onstage will often generate many notes, and it's critical the properties director be in attendance to assist with any adjustments or offer advice on prop use. When there is time, this first prop rehearsal is often done in what is called a *spacing rehearsal* without lights or sound but on the completed stage setting. The spacing rehearsal allows the director to make adjustments in the blocking and staging giving the actors an opportunity to experience the stage space in full light. This helps them understand how to move in the space both on stage and off. During the spacing rehearsal, all furniture should be in place onstage and the prop tables should be set up off stage with hand props available. The stage has at least the minimal dressing impacting the actor's entrances, exits, movement on the stage, or action. Hopefully, the stage masking is in place, and any light stands, speakers, or other technical support is in place allowing the actors to see travel paths backstage and know where it is safe to move and stand before entrance on the stage.

Prop department input in the collaborative problem-solving process with the director and designer is critical during this process of staging. Offering what can be done to make an action easier or suggesting options available when a prop is not working as hoped goes a long way to making the technical rehearsal process support the overall goal of creating a complete production. The intent is to be helpful, and each design/director team has a different dynamic. Some teams work in an open process accepting ideas from the technical staff, whereas others prefer to keep the discussion within the design team. The properties director probably has a notion of how to best present options based on prior interactions with the director and designers during the build process of the prior weeks. The properties director must always step in when a situation endangers the safety of people on stage or the integrity of a prop. Although the director may desire a specific action or visual, the properties director should suggest ways to handle or move props to insure the prop is not broken or damaged. If that is not possible, then the risk (and expense) of breakage should be discussed and evaluated in the context of budget, personnel, and time needed to repair or replace the prop if it should be damaged. Many stage directors are able to compromise to an action allowing for safe handling of the props on stage.

At the first full technical rehearsal when the elements of light, sound, and scene shifts are added, the spacing rehearsals value becomes evident, as many of the prop notes have already been solved. Those theatres lacking the time to have a spacing rehearsal will need to deal with prop notes in the technical rehearsal layered with the challenges from all the other areas.

Notes from the designer for additional toning or aging of props are common at the full technical rehearsal as the exposure of light makes evident the need for adjustment to color or distressing. A low light level or the length of scene change music complicates scene shifts that worked in full light without music. Actors suddenly have difficulty with a prop that worked the previous day. This is all normal and usual as the elements of technical storytelling layers onto the rehearsal process. Keeping a supportive and pleasant attitude to resolve the challenges helps make the time more useful and less stressful for all involved.

The properties director also assists in the scene change choreography to help insure the safety of the props and to suggest ways to assist in an efficient prop run. This might include providing a special padded box to assist with the safe removal of stemmed glassware, placing small tabs on a circular tablecloth to allow the scene shift person to feel where to place it on the table, or showing a crew person how to pick up a chair from the seat and *not* the arms. This process should always be worked out with the stage management person responsible for organizing the run crew.

Beyond working with the scene shift crew, the prop shop might be asked to work with an actor who has to handle a specific prop to help solve a particular problem or to show the actor the easiest way to manipulate the prop. If weapons are being used, the properties director should attend the first fight run through in the space to work in the safe coordination of the weaponry with the director and/or fight the choreographer in relation to the audience and stage setting. Most weaponry would have been used in rehearsal, so the adjustment is primarily to accommodate the use of the weapons now that the actors are in the theatre. All too often what was staged in the rehearsal hall requires adjustment and new choreography. The properties director should advocate for the appropriate use of the prop as well as any concerns about audience adjacency or safety.

As the technical rehearsal progresses, the properties director makes notes of things needing to be altered or requested "adds" or "cuts." By closely watching the play and how the props are used, often the properties director is able to make suggestions for simplifying or altering the way a prop is used in support of the full show experience. It may be something as simple as folding a letter smaller to allow the actor to access it from a costume pocket more easily or lining a tray with a non-slip surface to keep glasses from sliding around as the actor carries the tray. It might also be toning props down into the scenic palette or adding additional color or trim to a prop to connect it to a specific character or costume.

The designer may give notes as observed during the rehearsal or hand them all off at the end of the rehearsal. Many production teams utilize various online note sharing software to send notes during the rehearsal. All requests should be clarified and discussed with concerned parties along with any notes the properties director has made or received from the director, stage management, or actors. It isn't unusual for an actor to take the properties director aside to ask for a change to a prop without going through the standard protocol for such requests. These requests should be passed on to stage management, and all changes should be approved by the director or the designer before changing anything once the prop has been checked in and used on stage. Other production areas may make requests to the prop shop as well and those should be coordinated in the production meeting held at the end of the rehearsal.

Costumes are often added later in the technical rehearsal process bringing additional difficulties when the layers of wigs, make-up, and clothing go on the actors. Adjustments to hand props are common to accommodate a too small pocket or to allow a movement the costume requires. Even when a prop has worked previously, until all elements of the production process have been added, it's best to keep an open eye to the props and a generosity of spirit as to what might get added, changed, or cut.

There is generally a mini production meeting following each tech rehearsal attended by the director, production management, stage management, department heads, and designers. The purpose of this meeting is to communicate the notes, collaborate with other departments, confirm the following day's schedule and space usage, and prioritize use of the stage or notes to be taken care of before the next rehearsal. Problem solving in the group with all the production and design team available allows for the greatest collaboration to find solutions to any challenges occurring in the rehearsal. This process will continue at least through the first preview and in some cases all the way through opening. Stage management may publish production notes from these meetings and distribute them via email to be sure everyone is aware of changes, adds, priorities, and scheduling requests.

The prop artisans work to complete the requested changes or prop "fix" notes during the standard work call the following day. Letting stage management know when a prop has been removed from the storage cabinets in order for it to be worked on or altered is important. Many companies use a check-in/check-out system notating a props status on the door of the cabinet where the prop was stored. If the note requires painting or re-building, a sufficient dry/repair time should be planned for and an alternate rehearsal prop provided if the actual prop cannot be repaired, painted, altered, or fixed in time for it to be returned for the next technical rehearsal. Any new props added must be checked in to the run crew with stage management and appropriate notation on prop lists, storage cabinets, run tables, and tracking sheets completed.

By opening night, everything must work smoothly, and the technical rehearsal process is the time to work together to sort out what has to be get done, by whom, on what priority, and how. It is the best of times where all the areas of production mix together and create the world where the actors perform.

OPENING NIGHT/RUN

Opening night signals the point where the show leaves the "shop and build" process and is fully in the hands of stage management and the run crew. Daily performance reports (similar to rehearsal notes) are sent out to keep all areas informed of the status of the show. The *run crew* is responsible for maintaining the props and doing small repairs as necessary. The prop shop should provide cleaning supplies and instruct the crew on any specialty maintenance processes. Once the props reach the theatre, it is the responsibility of stage management and the props run crew to safely manage and maintain the props during the technical rehearsals, opening, and run of the show. Most theatres have a standard prop "run" protocol with established areas for the safekeeping of props as well as set locations for prop run tables.

In the event something major is broken or a repair is beyond the skill of the run crew, the prop is generally returned to the prop shop. Stage management should communicate immediately any problem requiring prop shop intervention and allowing adequate time for repair, replacement, or finding another solution before the call for next performance.

Running props during a show is an important part of the entire puzzle. Props must be placed for each performance in the same place each time, oriented in the same way, and ready to compete the action required. Workings with stage management, preset and tracking sheets are made allowing each prop to have a preset position on stage or on an offstage prop run table or cabinet. The tracking sheets follow each prop during the play and show any exits or entrances of the prop or if it requires a preset between scenes or acts in the play. It should also have a final track point where it can be found at the end of the play, even if it is only in a storage position in the prop run cabinet.

Prop run tables are usually set up in the wings or offstage areas of the stage allowing actors to easily find a prop adjacent to the entrance being utilized. Some organizations have prop run cabinets doubling as the prop lock-up for storage between shows. Whether using run tables or running out of the prop cabinet, these areas are usually labeled with the individual prop name and maybe even the scene used, allowing for quick and efficient prop set up and making it easy for the actor to find the prop in the same place for each performance.

The Skylight

The *Spitfire Grill* Show Run Sheet   Updated

6/14/08 MKH

PRESHOW DUTIES		
WHO	**WHAT**	**NOTES**
ANDREW	Unlock stage areas and dressing rooms, check crew sign-in, sweep/mop stage, help set needed furniture, unlock headsets, rail check, check in with PSM	
NIKKI	Check & set onstage & SR props	
ALEXIS/MAGGIE	Pick up artists, check & set SL props	
MICHELE	Set water stations & green room/coffee, check all presets, DND phone, report to PSM	
KOREN	Conduct dimmer check, report to PSM	
GARY	Check & set cast wireless mics, check any headset problems, report to PSM	
JUSTIN	Wardrobe presets, assist actors	
JANINE	Turn on spotlight, check in with crew chief	
TIM	Turn on spotlight, check in with crew chief	

TOP OF SHOW PRESET INFORMATION ***Italicized items are used in Act II only***

ONSTAGE		STAGE LEFT	STAGE RIGHT
Suitcase – Top Level	Butcher Block with: (DIAGRAM)	Lantern	Act II Tub #1 with:
Percy's Green Scarf – Costumes	*Top Shelf:*	Potato Bowl w. Peeler	Spice Rack
Percy's Blue Pea Coat – Costumes	Metal Oatmeal Pot w. Lid	Percy's Green Apron	Act II Salt Shaker
Bus Ticket in right pocket	2 Cast Iron Skillets	Egg Bowl	2 New Potholders
Picture of Gilead in left pocket	Act I Salt Shaker	Colander	2 New Kitchen Towels
Percy's Grey Sweatshirt inside Coat	*1st Shelf:*	Sack of Onions	Shelby Stack of Essays
Pack of Cigarettes in right pocket	Metal Baking Pan	Metal Lunch Box	Percy Stack of Essays
Stump – Down Right	*Bottom Shelf:*	White Phone	Hannah Stack of Essays
Axe – on the floor, right of stump	Secured Cutting Board	Cream/Brown Oatmeal Pot w. Lid	2 Blue Tin Cups
Rocking Chair	Oatmeal Canister w. Lid	Ketchup Refill Bottle & Rag	Jug
Wood Box full of wood	Stack of Small Bowls	Order Pad & Pencil	Act II Tub #2 with:
Hannah's Book w. Eyeglasses	Stack of Small Plates	Rolling Pin	Act II Coffee Pot
Shelby's Brown Apron	Pyrex Glass Measuring Cup	Flour Canister	3 Jars of Flowers
Counter with: (DIAGRAM)	Stack of Big Plates	Corn Husk Broom	2 Small Menus
Top Shelf:	Stack of Big Bowls	Hannah's Crutches	Cash Box w. Money
Cash Register	Trick Oatmeal Bowl – 2nd from top	Hannah's Cane	Candy Dish
Eraser	1 loose bowl on top of trick bowl	Gardening Hoe	2 Wrapped Aprons – Shelby on top
Act I Chalkboard	*Stage Right Side:*	Chains	Shelby Stack of Letters – 17 Letters
Order Keeper	2 Loose Act I Dish Towels – Blue	Ice Testing Rod	Shelby Final Essay
Jar of Pencils & Chalk	*Stage Left Side:*	Effy's Whistle	Percy Essay #1 (Green Folder)
Sugar Shaker	2 Act I Potholders	Recipe Card	Percy Final Essay
Creamer	Tray w. Utensils:	Effy Letter #1 – Philly w. Check	Effy Essays #2 & #3/Final
Order Pad & Pencil	Large Wooden Spoon	Effy Stack of Letters #2 – 8 Letters	Joe's Final Essay
Blank Order Pad	Spatula	- 8th w. $100 Bill	Hannah's Ad Newspaper w. Keys
1st Shelf:	2 Wire Whisks	Effy Stack of Letters #3 – 11 Letters	Percy's Prison File
Act I Coffee Pot	Blue Metal Spoon	Percy Stack of Letters – 12 Letters*	Joe's Coffee Cup
3 Bread with 3 Folded Towels	Fork on Top	2 Newspapers w. Spitfire Ads	Joe's Rolled Deed w. Red Ribbon
3 Cups w. Saucers	Tobasco Sauce	Xeroxed Newspaper Articles &	Eli's Feather
1 Cup w. No Saucer		Whisky Bottle	Eli's Bird
Stack of Silverware:	Stage Left Table w. 2 Chairs:	3 Letters for Joe	Joe's 2 Newspapers – Gilead Reporter
2 Knives, 2 Spoons, 2 Forks	2 Forks	Accordion Stack of Letters w. Effy	Cash for Joe's Tip
Record Ledger	2 Knives	Essay #1	Hannah's Ribbed Kitchen Towel
2nd Shelf:	2 Spoons	Joe Essays #1 & #2	Caleb's Phone
Plastic Water Pitcher, on its side	2 Cups w. Saucers-cups upside down	Hannah Essay	Axe Head, Sharpening Stone, Rag
Rag & Spray Bottle	2 Salt/Pepper Shakers	Shelby Essay	Caleb's Large Ratchet
Caleb's List of Supplies	Ketchup Bottle	Act II New Chalkboard	Road Salter
Dustpan & Whisk Broom	Napkin Dispenser - Full	White Blanket	Hannah's Blanket
Water Glass		Breakable Plate	Metal Bar for Top of Show
Bottom Shelf:	Stage Right Table w. 2 Chairs:	1 New Kitchen Towel	Pitch Pipe
2 Grey Bus Tubs – Empty	(SL Chair is throwable)	2 Rolls of Silverware	Box of Toothpicks
	2 Forks	$1 Bill for Effy's Tip	Effy's Shovel
Wire Wood Crate	2 Knives	3 Tablecloths – Ironed & Folded	Effy's Push Broom
2 Stools	2 Spoons	2 Pieces of Chalk	Black Fishing Pole
	2 Cups w. Saucers-cups upside down	Tissues for Effy	Empty Black Bin
	2 Salt/Pepper Shakers	4 Bags of Letters in Wheelbarrow	
	Ketchup Bottle	- Strings should be pulled tight	
	Napkin Dispenser	2 Sconces	
	Creamer		

RAIL:	ORCHESTRA PIT:		
Moon OUT	Sound FX Ratchet on Maestro Stand		

FIGURE 2 *Spitfire Grill* run sheets from Skylight Opera Production showing preshow duties for run crew and prop preset. Courtesy of Lisa Schlenker, Properties Director at Skylight Opera Theatre.

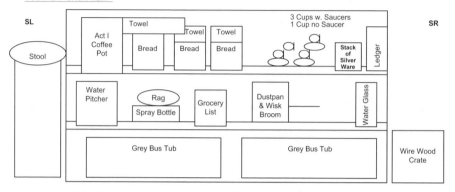

The^{The} Skylight *The Spitfire Grill Show Run Sheet*
ACT I DIAGRAMS:

COUNTER - BACK VIEW

NOTES:
- The Chalkboard is leaning against the Cash Register, with the Eraser between them.
- The stack of silverware should be able to all be grabbed in one hand
- Two of the coffee cups on saucers should be placed upside down. The third one on a saucer should be placed right side up.
- The towel on the SR loaf of bread is folded 2X. The middle and SL bread towels are folded 3X.
- The water pitcher should be placed sideways, with the handle pointed upstage, so it can be easily grabbed.

NOTE: Italicized Handoffs/Receives are where actors have a little bit of time to prep before their next entrance. These are not immediate.

ACT ONE = 1:05:00

WHEN	WHO	WHAT	NOTES
"Places"	ANDREW	SL	
	NIKKI	SR – Places for Orchestra, then RECEIVE: Pitch Pipe from PERCY SR	
	ALEXIS/MAGGIE	SL – ACTOR PLACES: HANNAH	
	MICHELE	SR – ACTOR PLACES: PERCY, JOE. ALSO: Preshow Speech Announcer	
	KOREN	Booth	
	GARY	Sound Booth	
	JUSTIN	Stage Right	
	JANINE	Spot #2	
	TIM	Spot #1	
SCENE 1 – *A Ring Around the Moon*			
00:00	MICHELE	SR3 - Bars	Q from PSM
	ANDREW	RAIL: Moon IN	Q from PSM
	NIKKI	SR2 - *HANDOFF: Coffee Cup & Percy File to JOE*	
	ANDREW	SL1 – HANDOFF: Lantern to HANNAH	
5:00	NIKKI	SR2 - RECEIVE: Coffee Cup & Percy File from JOE	
8:10	MICHELE	SR2 – HANDOFF: 2 Newspapers to JOE, RECEIVE: Lantern from HANNAH, TRACK Lantern to SL,	
	JUSTIN	**SR2 – RECEIVE: Blue Plaid Overshirt from HANNAH**	
9:15	ANDREW	SL1 – HANDOFF: Percy's Apron & Potato Bowl w. Peeler to HANNAH	
9:45	ALEXIS/MAGGIE	SL2 – RECEIVE: Coat, Scarf, Suitcase from PERCY	Warning from PSM
	NIKKI	SR Side Stage – STRIKE Bread & Towel, Remove axe from stump and set on the floor SR of stump	Warning from PSM
	ANDREW	RAIL – Moon (Line set #???) OUT	Q from PSM
SCENE 2 – *Something's Cooking*			
12:00	ANDREW	SL1 – HANDOFF: Egg Bowl to PERCY, RECEIVE: Cigarettes, Have Water Ready for PERCY	
13:05	ANDREW	SL1 – HANDOFF: Onion Sack to PERCY	
	ALEXIS/MAGGIE	*SL3 – HANDOFF: Lunchbox to SHELBY*	
16:00	ANDREW	SL1 – RECEIVE: Onion Sack from HANNAH	

FIGURE 3   Run crew sheet showing stage dressing placement and listing prop run handoffs and moves during the show for *Spitfire Grill*. Courtesy of Lisa Schlenker, Properties Director at Skylight Opera Theatre.

It is equally important for an area to be set aside for any prop to be dropped off by the actors as they exit the stage. On occasion, a prop must travel from where it is dropped off on one prop table to be preset again on a different prop table or a prop may get struck from where it is left onstage to return as a handoff later in the show. Under these circumstances, the prop run crew must know where and when the prop moves and designate a person to do it. As the scene shifts are choreographed, the tracking of the prop is incorporated in the shift, changes noted on the tracking/run sheets, and spaces made on prop tables to accommodate necessary placements or drop-offs.

Stage dressing for the top of the show or any placement of props done at intermission may require a deeper level of documentation to be sure everything is placed identically for each performance.

For those props set on stage, a hand sketched diagram may be created showing placement and noting any specific detail about placement. Digital photographs are an especially handy way of documenting as they can be easily updated during technical rehearsals when dressing evolves.

WEAPONS

Weapons require special consideration. Weapons should *never* be placed on prop run tables, but stored in a weapons lockup cabinet and handed off only as the actor prepares to go onstage. This prevents any accidental mishandling of the weapon especially in the case of a firearm when the weapon is fired. Guns loaded with stage blanks should follow a special high-security protocol to guarantee every precaution has been taken to insure the gun will fire as required and the actor using the gun, as well as anyone onstage when the gun is fired, has the assurance all established safety protocols have been followed keeping everyone safe. The coordination between stage management or run crew loading the gun and the handoff to the actor before entering the stage should be practiced as part of the technical rehearsal or during a fight call. The handoff of the weapon as the actor exits the stage and the safe securing of the weapon back into the weapons lock up must be coordinated between the actor, stage management, and the run crew. Under some circumstances, stage weapons such as a sword or a nonfiring gun are checked out to the actor at the top of the show, and it is the actor's responsibility to safeguard the weapon during the performance, checking it back in following curtain call. Under no circumstances should a weapon be stored in the dressing room with costumes as too many people have access leaving the weapon unsecured.

CONSUMABLES

Consumables (also called *perishables*) are the items used up, eaten, destroyed, broken, manipulated, or handled in such a way that they are good for only one performance. These items must be replaced every performance and an adequate supply provided to the run crew for the entire run of the show.

Consumable hand props can run the gamut from simple letters getting opened each night to pieces of pottery being thrown and smashed. Flower bouquets may need to be arranged with fresh flowers or candles

MILWAUKEE REPERTORY THEATRE
CYRANO CONSUMABLES LIST

PROP DIRECTOR, JIM GUY

#	Prop	Qty./Show	Who	Notes
P1103a	Wicks	3	Theatre Employees	For lighter snuffers, each snuffer will have a wick, only 3 will be used each show, Replace as necessary.
C1109	Oranges	1 to 3	Orange Girl (Ms. Silheimer)/Crowd/ Pickpocket (Mr. Knight)	1 Tossed into air, replace as necessary.
C1118	Macaroons	TBA	Orange Girl (Ms. Silheimer)/Crowd/ Cyrano (Mr. Ernst)	Broken in half and eaten by Mr. Ernst, sold to crowd
C1120	Grapes	3 bunches	Orange Girl (Ms. Silheimer)/Crowd/ Cyrano (Mr. Ernst)	One grape is eaten by Mr. Ernst, sold to crowd
P1236	Pie	1	Cyrano (Mr. Ernst), Musketeer (Mr. Neugent)	Mr. Neugent's face is smashed into a pie by Mr. Ernst, meringue
C1226c	Small Cakes	21-28	Poets	Consumed on stage
P1304	Candles (5)	10/run	Ms. Apalategui, Ms. Brennan, Ms.Beyer, Ms. Seilhelmer, Ms. Germany	Replace as necessary
P2505	Thread	1 spool/Run	Roxane (Ms. Partin)	Cut on stage, Rethread Needle (2505a) as necessary.
	Paper Props			
P1207	Brown Paper	1/show	Ragueneau (Mr. Hanson), Cyrano (Mr. Ernst)	Blank, at least one piece used per show
P1222	Paper cones (6)	12/wk	Lise (Ms. Apalategui), Ragueneau (Mr. Hanson) Poets	Begin flattened, will hold Pastries (#1202a). Replace as necessary.
P1222a	Recipe (1)	3-4/wk	Ragueneau (Mr. Hanson)	Folded into cone, unfolded on stage. Replace as necessary.
P1222b	Paper cones (2)	6-8/wk	Cyrano (Mr. Ernst), Duenna (Ms. Pickering)	One will hold 6 Cream puffs (#1212); one will hold 1 jelly roll (#1209); will begin open. Replace as necessary.
1222c	Paper cone-openable (1)	2/wk	Cyrano (Mr. Ernst), Duenna (Ms. Pickering)	Opened on stage by Cyrano (Mr. Ernst), Replace as needed.
1136	Folded note	2/wk	Duenna (Ms. Pickering)	Replace as necessary
1137	Crumpled scrap of paper	2/wk	Ligniere (Mr. Silbert)	Replace as necessary
P1226a	Loose Paper	1/show	Cyrano (Mr. Ernst)	Same stationary as Letter (#2404) and (#2508)
1302	Letter	2/wk	Ligniere (Mr. Silbert), Roxane (Ms. Partin)	Replace as necessary
2404	Letter	8/wk	Cyrano (Mr. Ernst), Christian (Mr. Martin)	Tri-folded and passed on stage, replace as necessary.
2508	Letter	2/wk	Roxane (Ms. Partin), Cyrano (Mr. Ernst)	Folded and placed in silk bag. Will be removed from bag on stage. Replace as necessary.

FIGURE 4   Consumable list for Milwaukee Repertory Theater's production of *Cyrano*. Courtesy of Jim Guy, Properties Director.

replaced in lanterns after burning down each night. Checking cigarette lighters for fuel, insuring the seltzer water dispenser is charged, and making tea sandwiches and tea; these all live on a "consumable" list. For consumables, it is usual to check in whatever is most convenient to be stored safely. In the case of a torn up letter, often an entire runs worth of letters can be checked in with the multiple copies in a clear plastic bag for safekeeping and labeled with the prop number. Larger items may require only a few items to be checked in and the run crew accesses the rest on an as-needed basis from the prop shop over the run.

Perishables such as food or fresh flowers are usually not checked in until later in the technical rehearsal time. Policies vary as to when food is introduced into the technical rehearsal process, but unless it is critical to the action of the scene, it is best to keep it until later rehearsals. Using food onstage during technical rehearsals is especially problematic as the length of the scenes are often not true to the actual action causing food to set longer in preset or under the lights onstage as various technical problems are worked out. For this reason, food is often not introduced until the technical rehearsals are able to move at a "run" pace.

Food preset backstage should be appropriately stored safe from tampering by others and with appropriate refrigeration/heat. If food must be cooked or otherwise "handled," a safe food handling area must be provided to guarantee the food is kept at a safe temperature and free from contamination during the preparation time.

Food and drink props require special concern and handling. Anticipating difficulties, stage management should determine any special requests or allergy preferences when actors are required to consume food or drink liquid on stage. Some people will not eat meat, and if their part requires them to consume a meat sandwich, then a substitution must be found. Many actors also prefer to only consume easily chewed and swallowed food. It would be rare to have peanut butter, making it difficult for the actor to speak or crumbly dry crackers making a mess on stage. Many performers also prefer low fat or diet foods. Decaffeinated coffee and tea are usually preferred. It is common to substitute plain water tinted with caramel coloring or food coloring for wine or other alcoholic beverages. Special thought should be given to what and how much an actor will eat on stage. Many scenes requiring food can be supported by a minimal quantity of actual food consumption.

For example, scenes set in Victorian times often have tea served, and although an entire tea service may be presented, the sandwiches and other items may all be fake with only a single plate of cookies being edible, giving the necessary visual appearance required by the script, but limiting the action to easily consumed and managed food. Other plays such as *The Art of Dining*, set in a restaurant kitchen where actors must prepare and cook full meals that are then served in the restaurant's dining room to other actors acting as patrons of the restaurant, requires an entirely different approach. The provision for that level of consumables is enormous and requires considerable forethought and an appropriate level of funding to comply with safe food handling rules and regulations, as well as appropriate training of the actors preparing the food, and of the run crew in preset and postshow handling of the food, and cleaning of the stage kitchen area.

Often prop food is entirely faked. Styrofoam and plaster can be made up to create beautiful pastries. Rubber bands painted beige make realistic noodles. Fish and poultry can be carved from foam and painted to look like a completed dinner entre. If the show has a short run, oftentimes, the food can be real food, refrigerated at the end of each performance, and disposed of at the end of the run. The expense of buying real food and using it over and over, when *not* consumed, is often a more cost-effective option than the time and expense of manufacturing fake food. However, it is of critical importance that everyone, including the crew, understands that the food is a prop and not to be consumed because the food might not be safe after being out under stage lights for several performances.

When any food is eaten onstage, it must be kept at safe storage temperature, and any food handled should be dealt with in ways guaranteeing the safety and good health of those who may eat the prop. Many regional theatres provide a prop run room including a prop kitchen with refrigerator, stove, microwave, and sinks, allowing for the safe storage, preparation, and run of prop food. When a prop run kitchen is not available, a separate clean "kitchen" run space should be set up.

Having a list of all the consumable/perishable items needed to be replaced, fixed, checked, or "made/cooked" helps the run crew keep an accurate way of knowing they have adequate supplies on hand and can quickly communicate any needs to the prop shop when supplies run low.

PERSONALS

Some items are considered "personal" props, and those props are often checked in to the actor at the start of the technical rehearsal process and may be stored in the dressing room with the costume. Examples of these kind of personal props would include an eyeglass case, paper money or coins, a cane or umbrella, a cigarette lighter or case, or a holster for a gun. If kept in the dressing room, they should become part of the costume run crews check list and are the responsibility of the costume run crew. These items are checked back in to the prop shop at strike.

If no costume run crew is available, it is wise to have these items tracked by stage management or the run crew during the run of the show with the understanding that the prop is checked back into prop storage and then preset in the dressing room not simply left in the dressing room. This is the preferred method, as all too often these props tend to be the ones that go missing if simply left in the dressing room with the make-up and costumes.

RUN STORAGE

Safe and secure storage of props between show performances is a critical part of a prop run crew. Many organizations have a room to temporarily store the hand props and stage dressing struck from the set following the performance. Some dressing can be left in place, but any prop critical to the action of the play should be struck for safekeeping to either a lockable prop run cabinet or to the prop run room. Any cleaning of props should be completed immediately following the show including weapon maintenance, washing of glassware or dishes, laundry of towels or other soiled soft goods, and wiping down of tables and counter tops. This is especially important when special effects such as blood are used. Stage blood is difficult to remove when dry and will stain fabric or painted surfaces if not cleaned up immediately following the performance. Storage of prop furniture and large items must be coordinated with the stage crew, and if scenery is being flown in/out or a slip stage is utilized, special consideration for the safety of the props is needed to prevent accidental crushing offstage. At the end of each performance, all furniture should be covered with muslin dust covers to discourage anyone from sitting on or moving the pieces as well as to keep the items clean.

PERFORMANCE REPORTS

At the end of each performance, stage management completes a performance report sent out to area heads, administration, and anyone else who needs to know the information in the report. This report usually includes the following information:

- Name of the show
- Date and curtain time
- Act timings/run time
- Performance notes about anything that occurred during the play such as incorrect presets, accidents, slow pacing, missed cues, etc.
- Actor notes such as missed entrances, dropped lines, or "off" delivery
- Production notes such as broken props, headset difficulties, maintenance issues, costumes needing repair or adjustment, and any technical difficulties encountered by the run crew.

The production notes section is where the properties director is notified of anything dealing with props and determines whether the run crew will be able to fix or adjust the prop and whether the prop shop should take over repair. It is also where the stage management alerts the prop shop when food or other consumables are running low and need to be replenished.

It is common practice to have some sort of system to "check out" and "check in" props requiring maintenance or repair. Some companies utilize a simple notation system on the storage cabinet. If a larger item such as furniture requires removal from the space, notification is often done via email with appropriate follow-up on the status of the piece. Any prop removed for maintenance or repair should be returned in adequate time to allow for proper check in and placement by the run crew for the next performance. If an item is damaged beyond immediate repair (or lost), the prop shop will need to provide an adequate substitute allowing the performance to run unhindered, hence the importance of a detailed and immediate performance report to all areas needing to respond to a problem. In the case of disaster striking, a phone call to the properties director immediately following the performance can assist in more prompt action rather than waiting until the following day when the performance report is read at the start of the work day.

STRIKE

Strike is the reverse of load-in when all elements for a production are removed from the theatre for the next production to begin load-in. At many theatres, strike begins immediately following the final performance. Some organizations prefer to schedule strike the following day, and in that case, the props should be stored in their normal and usual show run storage position unless other arrangements have been made with the prop department.

During strike, all props and set dressing must be removed to facilitate other department's strikes and to guarantee the safety of the props. Usually the prop crew is the first on stage to remove their items as the other areas clear backstage areas and prepare for the load-out. To facilitate all areas and allow the strike to progress without delay, dressing items are often temporarily removed to a secure area, backstage, where they can be later packed in boxes or placed onto a cart for return to the prop shop for cleaning and final storage or disposal. Furniture is removed from the stage, often to an area adjacent to or in the loading dock allowing for transportation to storage. Hand props are loaded into boxes and returned to the prop shop. Personal props stored with the costumes are picked up from the dressing rooms or costume shop.

Once all stage props have been cleared, the scenery and electrics strike can continue without fear of damaging the props and without the prop crew being onstage when lights are flown in or large scenic pieces are being torn apart and removed. This is for the safety and security of the crew as well as the props. Flown props such as chandeliers or dressing on flown scenic items are removed as the pieces become available during the strike. The electrics crew usually removes any additional wiring apparatus or rigging prior to returning items to the prop shop following strike.

A written strike plan aids in completing an organized and efficient strike giving each artisan a list of specific responsibilities during the strike by priority of what needs to happen in coordination with the other production areas.

Following strike, all prop rentals and borrowed items need to be returned. All stock props should be cleaned or laundered before returning to stock. This is especially critical for items that have been in contact with food, been contaminated during the action of the play, or may have utilized floral putty or other substances to secure set dressing.

White Christmas Prop Department Strike Plan

Immediately post show, On Stage and in wings:
With Prop Run Crew:

> Move all furniture pieces from stage & wings to loading dock area of scene shop, and check them in on master storage list
> Check all hand props and Inn desk dressing back into prop boxes for transport to storage
> Collect, wash & dry dirty dishes, check in to prop box
> Gather soiled linens, take upstairs to prop shop for laundering

With Stage Management:

> Clear personal props from dressing rooms to prop boxes

With Scene shop strike crew:

> Roll Train Wagon into Scene Shop space for later disassembly
> Roll WWII unit into Scene shop space for later disassembly
> Fly in Inn wall, remove dressing, drapery, and fixtures; check in and bag or box appropriately
> Fly in Inn Chandelier, disconnect from rigging and unplug power supply,
>> Transfer to rolling storage rack for loading onto truck

First Priority off deck:
Lisa and Jen: Unbolt and remove train benches from wagon unit

> Remove curtains and valences from train flat and bag for storage

With Electrics staff:

> Disconnect power to Train unit sconces and Army drop lighting
> Remove wall sconces and box for storage

Brian, Ana & Meghan: Bag army Xmas tree, Inn Xmas tree, Chorus Xmas all six Finale Xmas trees

> Begin dismantling the army drop unit for storage

Second Priority:
Lisa: With Sound Crew:

> Disconnect and remove speakers and wireless equipment from both prop piano units

Brian: pull box truck into loading dock; load furniture

Third Priority:
All Prop Personnel: transport all White Christmas from scene shop to warehouse.
Meghan: Do White Christmas prop laundry and shelve run crew supplies back in to prop shop stock.

FIGURE 5   Strike plan for Skylight Opera's production of *White Christmas* showing the specific duties of each artisan and the priorities for prop removal and coordination with other production areas. Courtesy of Lisa Schlenker, Properties Director at Skylight Opera Theatre.

Soft goods should be laundered, china and dishes washed, furniture wiped down or vacuumed as needed, and weapons cleaned and oiled. All props should be returned to their proper storage location, and if a prop inventory is maintained, it should be updated to reflect the most recent adds, alterations, or cuts. Items borrowed from costumes for dressing should be laundered as needed and returned to the costume shop.

In the case of some shows stored for a re-mount at a later date or traveling to another theatre, the show will need to be packed in an appropriate way. If the items are boxed, label the box with the name of the show, include an inventory on both the inside and the outside of the box, and mark which side is up. For larger items such as furniture or dressing items, it is handy to sew lightweight muslin covers stenciled with the show name to be tied over the piece to keep off dust. All pieces needing to be loaded into a truck or moved should be well padded and secured to protect the integrity of the prop. Props returning for re-mount such as *A Christmas Carol*, which many theatres run each winter, may be stored in a separate storage area, often with the scenery and not mixed in with the usual prop stock. Making sure the props are safely stored and covered to keep clean and secure from accidental damage is important. Props being sent on for use in a co-production may be boxed, labeled, and put on a palette or in a moving container for transportation to the next site. Larger items should be appropriately covered, padded, and secured before loading or shipping.

Following opening, the properties director should complete the show "bible" with the preset and run lists, perishable checklist, photos of the show and set dressing, and all final notes and responses. This allows a record to be maintained about the show, and information can be easily accessed in the case of a remount, co-production or transfer, or when questions about research, sources, or processes arise. Following strike, the show bible is closed with a final accounting on the budget and rentals. Retention of show bibles or keeping a show file on the shop computer allows easy access to the production history and is a valuable resource.

Each season brings its own unique set of prop challenges. Each build is as ephemeral as some of the props used on the stage, lasting for a markedly brief time. Working props in the theatre and creating the small worlds on stage can be an immensely rewarding career. Each show opens the mind to a different time, different characters, new solutions, old problems, and always a chance to discover the "What if...?" It does take a certain open and artistic mind-set, devoid of ego, and comfortable with adaptability and change. Whether managing a shop or creating the smallest of props, the properties director must utilize the highest level of grace and integrity coupled with creativity and understanding of the play. May the theatre continue to provide entertainment, challenge our minds, and touch our hearts and may this book have given some level of understanding behind the scenes into the prop shop and managing a prop build.

Chapter 9

The Prop Shop

Tools, Supplies, Space, and Storage

To be an effective prop director and manage a build creatively, a designated workspace is required—the prop shop! During production work, the prop shop supports an enormous number of different activities. The prop shop does wood, plastics, foam, and metal work similar to the scene shop; sewing, draping, dyeing, and distressing work similar to the costume shop; and painting, finishing, and crafting similar to what is completed in the scenic paint shop. This overlap of skill sets and processes generates a challenge in creating a functional prop shop and has historically forced the prop shop to work scattered about the other theatre shops with only a small space designated for props. Given the fairly recent history of having props identified as its own separate craft, the common way of working was often to simply have a corner of the scene shop for prop construction and all other work was done in whatever clean nook or cranny could be found for craft work and soft goods. That worked in a limited way depending on the space available, but all too often usually to the dissatisfaction of the props crew as well as the other theatre craftspeople trying to do their own work.

As the expense of producing massive scenic units increased and performance spaces evolved bringing the thrust stage out and up close to the audience, the use of props to establish the scene increased the need to support the prop shop differently. Just as the identification of a separate staff to build props has become the industry standard so has supporting a shop space dedicated to the production of props.

In an ideal theatre world, the prop shop would be clean, safe, and spacious. It would have good illumination including some natural light, adequate ventilation and dust collection, designated work spaces appropriate to the processes and products used, an organized tool and materials storage, easy access to a loading dock for materials and large prop deliveries, adjacent access to hand/furniture/dressing prop storage, a secure and separate space for an office, and adjacency to other production spaces and personnel.

Many theatres undergo the acquisition or renovation of spaces, but all too often the production spaces fall secondary to the public spaces and the level of planning and space allocation needed to function well is inadequate. Production shop requirements often disappear when budget and space determine other priorities. It is critical that the voice of the artisans who spend hours upon hours in these spaces be heard, and the needs and safety of these people considered in the planning of these production facilities and renovations of existing theatre spaces. Professional and creative work can be best accomplished when given pleasant and safe working environments. It's also important to maintain the space and keep the functionality flexible to encompass the wide variety of projects completed in the prop shop. Shops should be analyzed periodically for safer ways of working, better utilization of space, appropriate storage of products and finished props, or easier communication between the staff. By advocating for a worker-friendly shop and setting up the space so that work can be completed efficiently and safely, the prop shop can be a healthy and pleasant work environment.

Given the various and, at times, conflicting projects needing to be accomplished on any given build, having adequate space designated by function is important in setting up a prop shop. The prop shop must function as a wood and metal construction shop, costume shop, crafts shop, paint shop, graphics shop, floral shop, and on and on through all the various skill sets. These areas do *not* always function well together and indeed may create havoc in the work processes if attempted in the same space at the same time. Sawdust and fabric do not work well together. Curing molds and castings can create irritating outgases for artisans working on other projects. Completed props stored for check-in can be damaged or become dirty if not protected from the building process.

Given the need to house so many different kinds of processes and products, the prop shop needs to be a flexible workspace allowing the show needs to be accommodated. Defining the space to suit the required work is critical. These spaces may be actual physically separate rooms or may be contained within one large shop divided into separate contained work areas. The properties director's job of managing the spaces and directing the personnel is simplified if the areas are easily accessible or at least adjacent to each other. Defining workspaces allows project work to continue without creating overlap of space, tools, or product impact on other projects.

Larger regional theatres have spaces that are divided into several zones of activity. These are known within the business as a "dirty" room, "clean" room, and often a "crafts" room. Smaller theatres may not have separate rooms for these activities, but incorporate the work within one larger space utilizing temporary setups to create the same work environments.

THE MULTIPLE-SPACE SHOP

The *dirty room* is primarily a woods and metal working space. In addition to the standard table saw, radial arm, band saw, etc. of a scene shop, a prop shop will have some tools more specific to furniture construction like a power miter saw, wood lathe, vacuum form, shaper, planer, jig saws, and various hand tools allowing for a finer level of detail and higher level of craftsmanship. A wide variety of clamps also offer solutions to the more unusual gluing and clamping challenges seen in prop construction and furniture work.

The activities in this shop include furniture construction, stripping, restoration, metal reinforcement, plastics work, foam carving, and other processes generating dust, smoke, dirt, or fumes. Dirty rooms often have a dust collection system to keep the sawdust generated by the woodworking process to a minimum. Documentation shows that saw dust can be irritating to the lungs of many workers creating a cumulative allergic reaction over time as well as being a potential explosive hazard. A dust collection system on tools and a continuous dust filtration system pulling dust particles from the air make for a safer and healthier shop.

FIGURE 1 Dust collection hookups to stationary tools keep the shop clean and safe. Courtesy of Seattle Children's Theatre.

In consideration of where to place the prop shop in the building, direct access is important for loading in raw materials as well as the delivery of props from the shop to the stage space. Some prop shops have the luxury of direct access to an external loading dock, whereas others utilize a freight elevator to move items to the prop shop location. Using a passenger elevator to move large items, especially lumber, is not a good idea. Passenger elevators are rated for moving people not plywood or sofas. Some prop shops located on floors above the street level lacking access to a freight elevator may have to carry supplies up the stairs and then carry the finished props down to the theatre. This obviously should be avoided when planning a prop shop. Anticipate how carts can roll from the access point to the prop shop saving time, effort, and the physical health and morale of the prop staff.

Inside the prop shop, adequate flat storage for plywood, lumber, metal, and plastics should be provided. Wood stocked in the prop shop needs to be more select than what is usually found in the scene shop allowing for strong joints and clear runs on furniture pieces. Poplar, ash, and birch are often used for prop furniture construction. Pine (clear, select) can be used for framing, but it is important to keep knots to a minimum. Hard woods such as oak, walnut, or cherry are too expensive and too heavy for most prop work, but may be used for trim or for turned pieces. Plywood with a faced surface such as oak-faced or birch-faced plywood offer the look of hardwood with the strength, durability, and ease of working associated with plywood.

FIGURE 2 Lumber stock stored above the miter saw allows for easy access. Scraps are placed underneath in the rolling cart for disposal. Tools and supplies are stored in the cabinets beneath the saw table. Courtesy of Seattle Children's Theatre.

An organized storage for fasteners and supplies such as staples, bolts, nails, screws, brads, hinges, glues, molding, sandpaper, etc. assists the build process. Fasteners in the prop area include more furniture specialized items such as biscuits, table lags, and doweling. Hardware tends to be smaller and often more decorative in nature than the items found in the scene shop.

Most regional theatre shops work off a pneumatic system powering the various staple guns and brad nailers used in the prop shop. If the building is not supplied with an in-house system, then an adequately sized compressor must be installed. An adequate amount of electrical circuits and wall outlets allows flexible use of power hand tools such as drills, sabre saws, or routers. The safety hazard of cords running across the floor can be minimized by the installation of pneumatic and electrical cords able to be pulled down from overhead reels or with the installation of floor pockets near stationary tools.

Prop shop metal working areas often have a standard metal inert gas welder for most mild steel welding with an aluminum spool gun attachment to allow for construction of lighter weight or structural yet decorative elements utilizing aluminum. For larger

FIGURE 3 Metalworking area in the "dirty room" at Milwaukee Repertory Theater's prop shop.

jobs, an oxy-acetylene rig for braising metals and cutting is used. Appropriate venting and fire-resistant floor protection should be provided.

Appropriate cutting and finishing tools such as chop saws, portable-band metal cutting band saws, grinders, wire wheels, buffers, pneumatic nibblers for delicate or small scale grinding and metal shaping applications, benders for small-scale steel stock, vices, etc. are needed. A metal table or cement slab for project work with a welding shield screen and appropriate ventilation makes it a safer process. Personal safety equipment such as welding gloves, fume respirators, face masks, etc. should be provided. Smaller projects utilize smaller propane or gas torches for sweating copper and tiny butane torches for high-temperature soldering requirements. Certainly, some prop shops will share welding facilities with the scene shop, but increasingly, prop shops are investing in designated equipment to meet more specialized metal construction requirements. Stock materials in the prop metal working area are again typically smaller in scale and more delicate than the corresponding structural components in the scenic department, although it is common for some furniture pieces used vigorously to require steel structural reinforcement from the prop department on par with scenic construction techniques in steel.

The *clean room* is designated for fabric layout, draping, and upholstery-related tasks, paper goods and floral projects, graphics work, set-dressing modification, some crafts work, and other activities that require a space free from air-born contaminants or dust.

The graphics area requires a computer with a scanner and wide-frame printer for creation, alteration, and printing of photos, money, legal documents, etc. supplemented by a drafting/light table for lay out work by hand. Computers today are evolving so quickly, and the software being developed that the level of ephemera able to be created is really only limited by the skill of the artisan with an understanding of programs such as Adobe Photoshop and Adobe Illustrator to name just two in a field of many. Access to the web allows for the downloading of images for easy manipulation and printing for stage use. Document creation has been revolutionized, and many prop items requiring hours of hand work in past years are now completed with the click of a computer mouse.

The upholstery and soft goods process utilize much of the same equipment similar to the costume shop but require machines able to handle drapery and upholstery weight materials. In addition to heavy-duty sewing machines, most shops have a serger or marrow machine, an ironing table with industrial steam iron, patterning tables with surfaces allowing fabric to be pinned down, and sewing hand tools such as scissors, measuring tapes, tack hammers, tufting needles, pattern weights, etc.

FIGURE 4   Seattle Children's Theatre "clean room" for soft goods and craftwork.

For doing upholstery and other types of theatrical or heavyweight fabrics, a walking-foot sewing machine is often used. A *walking-foot sewing machine* has a special pressure foot operating in two parts to pull or "walk" the fabric through the machine allowing multiple layers of fabric or heavy weight fabric to be more easily sewn. This is especially useful when doing stage draperies. Having the machine inset into a large worktable assists in the handling of the material as it is walked through the machine.

The prop shop *upholstery area* ideally has a variety of webbing stretchers, pneumatic long-nose staple guns, tack pullers, and an electric foam saw. Long nose staple guns allow upholstery fabric to be easily stapled deep in the folds and crevices of furniture. A foam saw is a long-bladed saber saw type of tool with a rolling base allowing upholstery foam to be cut with square edges and following patterned shapes.

Upholstery and drapery supplies include cotton and polyester batting, muslin and cambric, foam rubber in various densities and thicknesses, spray adhesives, heavy-duty thread, tying twine, decorative gimp and fringes, drapery tape and webbing as well as various fasteners such as staples, webbing tacks, and decorative nail strips. Just as in the "dirty" shop, appropriate electrical and pneumatic outlets should be provided to minimize the use of extension cords, and ventilation filtering should be used to minimize the effects of dander, dust mites, mold, hair, and other "nitty gritties" found in furniture when being reupholstered.

FIGURE 5 Craft dye room and paint area for Milwaukee Repertory Theater's prop shop.

Many upholstery and soft goods areas also have adjacent fabric cleaning and dyeing/distressing areas with an industrial washer and reversible dryer. Often this area is incorporated in a *crafts room*. The crafts room falls somewhere between the two other spaces supporting the wide variety of craft work done in the prop shop. It generally incorporates the "wet" and "hazardous" activities.

The crafts room often has a large steam vat for dye work (preferably stainless steel), dye mixing area with a stove or hot plate for heating water for dye solutions with a ventilation grill to pull dye fume away from the work area, a walk-in spray booth for exhaust of paint and curing materials, and a paint/plaster sink. The spray booth and dye ventilation system allow contaminated air to be removed from the work area and exhausted via a filtering system to the outside. Any spray painting or work with finishes emitting an odor or fume should be done in this ventilated space; hence, adequate size and ease of entry are important considerations. The prop shop utilizes spray paint and spray finishes more than any other area in the theatre due to the highly detailed nature of many of the items. In some shops, depending on the size of the unit, make up air may need to be installed to balance the room airflow.

Appropriate safety cabinets are necessary to store the flammable liquids (acetone, denatured alcohol, shellacs, mineral spirits, etc.) and paints used in props work. Like the scenic paint studio, water-soluble latex or acrylic paint and glaze materials are standard for prop shop painting supplemented by pure pigments for mixing into the glaze, dyes for French enamel varnish work (FEV), bronzing powders, and gold leaf. Supplies often include a wide variety of buckets and pails, brushes, wood combs, sponges, and specialty faux painting tools.

FIGURE 6 Storage of paint and flammables in a safety cabinet insures a safe workspace. Courtesy of Milwaukee Repertory Theater.

The crafts area usually has several tables for working on the wide variety of projects needed in props crafts work. Having at least one table with a stainless steel top is handy when working with dyes and on casting and molding projects where keeping a clean surface is important as well as allowing easy cleanup.

The crafts room also might contain an area where furniture can be "stripped." This requires an area where entire furniture pieces can be covered with stripper and allowed to rest while the stripper works to dissolve the paint back to bare wood. Most pieces being stripped require vigorous washing, so having a hose and large chemical floor drain accommodating the dissolved paint and stripper is helpful.

Besides the usual hand tools, specialty tools and supplies include corner and small hand clamps for custom picture framing and small construction or repair of hand props, small watercolor and acrylic paint brushes and paints for touch-up and re-paint of pulled hand props, an airbrush for detail work, floral wire, tape and putty for creating silk floral arrangements, a variety of markers, sealers, and paper or parchments in different colors and weights for making ephemera. Molding and casting supplies might include mixing cups, stir sticks, a scale, Teflon pans, plaster, spray releases, a hot plate for melting materials, silicon spatulas, plastic tubs, and aluminum sheet pans. Standard supplies for this area include plaster, tape, glue, spray sealers, stamps, and seals.

THE SINGLE-SPACE SHOP

Some regional theatre and university prop shops are small multifunctional spaces requiring a juggling of processes and setups to allow for the widest variety of work to be accomplished. Managing the flow of materials and work processes within a single space that must manage the "dirty" side of prop work from woodworking and foam carving to "clean" activities such as upholstery and floral work adds complexity to an already complicated job. In these one-room shops, the table saw lives with the sewing machine, the paint sink doubles as the area where props are washed and cleaned, and the shop graphics computer area is often the properties director's desk.

FIGURE 7   Single-space prop shop. Courtesy of Intiman Theatre, Seattle.

When possible, shops should have some method of defining and isolating work areas allowing for the safe and appropriate use of materials and work processes, but given the reality of most spaces, this is accomplished with limited success. Sawdust, paint spray, upholstery lint, wet glues and finishes, damp dyed fabric, noisy sawing, castings releasing gases, and the jumble of stock supplies all must thrive in the single-space prop shop. Work may be compromised, and the functionality of the prop shop limited simply by the need to constantly prioritize projects depending on how much space they require, how much of a mess (dust, fume, over-spray, lint, trash, gas, etc.) will be created, drying time, etc. As projects flow through the shop, work spaces must be adaptable for a variety of projects with the prop artisans determining what projects need priority in the build and what other projects compliment the same use of tools, products, or process.

Just as in the multiple-space prop shop, the one-room shop probably has a division of the space into working areas replicating the clean, dirty, and crafts rooms. Some overlap, and duel usage occurs naturally as the build progresses through the shop, but many one-room prop shops have artisans with multiple skills allowing the shop to change as the project they are working on moves from start to finish. The same concerns for isolation for dust, contamination, fume, etc. should be

addressed, and temporary barriers, mobile work tables, tools on rolling stands, and flexible systems for ventilation and dust collection can
help make the shop function quite well for properties production.
Simple solutions such as storing supplies in plastic containers with
secure lids, providing dust covers over prop storage shelves and dust-
sensitive equipment such as sewing machines or computers, or even
rigging a physical barrier to temporarily divide the shop as needed
give the shop functionality. Keeping an organized shop is critical in the
one-room prop shop to keep a safe work area and managing tools and
supplies. When specialty artisans work in designated multiple-room
prop shops, they are able to individualize their areas to their work
style and manage the area worked in to suit their own process. Not
so in a one-room shop where the artisans often take projects from
beginning to end and the spaces and tools are shared. Attention to
safety and the requirements of specific processes must be part of each
artisan's work plan.

   In the case where space is really limited, the prop artisans may share
workspace with other production shops. For example, furniture construction or metal reinforcement of props may occur in the scene shop
allowing for similar material use and the mess of cutting, sanding, and
grinding in a space set up to accommodate that activity. The prop staff
may find clean space in the scenic paint studio to paint, stain, and seal
furniture or props side by side with the artisans completing the scenery.
This has the added benefit of allowing collaboration on style and color
palette in addition to having an environment safe from the dust and
residue of construction work. The costume shop may allow the props
artisan to complete a drapery project requiring a clean workspace with
the use of a large cutting table and industrial sewing machine. Many
smaller companies have a shared area for the costume and prop shop
to do fabric washing and dye work. Administration, marketing, design,
and production may share expensive specialty equipment, such as a
wide-frame color plotter, allowing the prop shop to produce posters
and large graphics, but not have the expense of the machine totally on
the prop shop.

   As with all shared resources, this way of working requires the willing
collaboration of all departments and the allowance of each shop's

activities to continue while accommodating the other shop's needs. Many theatres operate on increasingly limited budgets, and when it is possible to share equipment or space, the overall benefits are increased collaboration and smart use of resources allowing the budget to be spent on more show specific purchases.

PROP STOCK AND STORAGE

Having a space set aside for the organized and safe storage of prop items allows a huge cost savings to the theatre company. Being able to utilize items purchased for previous shows or to modify existing furniture items for use onstage saves hundreds of dollars as well as hours of labor otherwise used to find and procure the items. Most theatres have a storage area for both large set props, mostly furniture pieces, as well as storage for hand props and dressing items.

Some theatres have the good fortune to have storage adjacent to the prop shop allowing easy access to stock, but all too often the props are stored off-site in a warehouse or other location. This makes for greater difficulty in knowing what is available for use or what the items look like unless some kind of inventory or photo library showing the items has been created. It can also add transportation issues for moving the items to and from the theatre.

In prop land, a wide variety of items need to be stored, and the odd shapes of things can take up a lot of storage space. Knowing what to keep and what to throw away is a constant juggle. The properties director must consider what kind of shows the theatre usually produces and the viability of each prop to return for use in the future. Keeping items in storage of a highly specialized nature is not usually worth it unless the theatre can rent them out to others and justify the expense of storing it.

Managing the prop stock is an enormous responsibility, and keeping an inventory of the items for easy access is a helpful tool when planning a prop build. An inventory system for the furniture and set pieces is especially helpful with out of town designers who are unable to walk through storage and see the items. The prop director can scroll

FIGURE 8 Seattle Repertory Theatre's furniture prop storage.

through the inventory narrowing the selection of available pieces for the designer to view via the web or utilizing a photo-sharing program like Dropbox. Most organizations have some kind of inventory of their set props, but it is unrealistic to do a hand prop and dressing inventory simply due to how many items it would include as well as how often these items are modified, broken, or thrown away after using in a show.

Many organizations have a set props space utilizing stacked storage racks to maximize the space available. Larger items such as sofas and tables are on the floor under the upper racks holding side tables, chairs, benches, and other lighter weight or more easily maneuvered items. Rugs are often stored rolled and hung from a pipe system with tags available to show size and a photo for understanding color and pattern. Set prop storage is often organized by "kind" rather than by "period." All the benches are together. The sofas are grouped near each other. The chairs are stacked in sets and often arranged by time period or "look." Kitchen items like refrigerators, stoves, and sinks are clustered together. The really odd items like dead animals, luggage, lamps and chandeliers, trees and floral, barrels and crates, or electrical/TV/radios often have their own designated area.

FIGURE 9 Hand prop storage for Seattle Repertory Theatre's prop shop.

Hand props and set dressing props are often re-used on stage, and an efficient storage system is extremely helpful to assist in the "pull" of those items. Keeping tablecloths, towels, draperies, or other fabric items in clear plastic boxes with lids and clearly labeled ends helps keep them clean and easily accessible. China, glassware, silverware, and serving dishes are often stored on shelves grouped according to pattern or kind. Weapons storage or valuable items should have extra security precautions, usually accomplished by a separate room with limited access. Books can be stored in boxes by kind or size. Further designation by hardcover or paperback, religious or secular, or textbook is common. Ephemera such as magazines, postcards, newspaper, calendars, or letters are easily stored in file cabinets divided in folders. Keeping the paper goods made for one show in a large envelope labeled with show name allows easy access when a similar paper prop is needed or the props can be separated out into subcategories such as letters, lists, receipts, contracts, menus, etc.

Most hand prop storage areas also include floral storage with flowers kept in storage boxes divided by color or kind. Some shops keep floral arrangements intact after use on stage, whereas others prefer to pull them apart and store the flowers separate from the vases. A vast array of items for filling shelves and decorating the set can take up yards of shelf space and fill the walls. Picture frames, clocks, decorative pottery, typewriters, lamps and lanterns, ashtrays, fake food, body parts, buckets and boxes, candlesticks and candles, religious icons, posters, pillows … the list is endless. Unfortunately, storage is limited. The juggle of what to keep and what to throw away is a constant concern. Planning for adequate storage and maintaining a prop stock is a necessity for a well-run prop shop as well as a tremendous asset for the producing organization.

For more information on how to plan a prop shop and to learn more about shop safety, ventilation, electrical and lighting, dust collection, floor and wall treatments, tag-out/lock-out, and other prop shop management issues or to view photo albums of props shops from around the United States, please go to my website: prophandbook.com.

Appendix

For those folks interested in exploring more about this theatre specialty or to learn about how to set up a prop shop and see photos of prop shops around the United States, please view my webpage: prophandbook.com.

For more information on how to build props and the skills of a props artisan, I recommend *The Prop Building Guidebook* by Eric Hart published by Focal Press.

For more information on Society of Properties Artisans/Managers, please go to the webpage: http://propmasters.org.

Index